COLLEGE

RE

STRATEGIC PROCUREMENT MANAGEMENT

CONCEPTS AND CASES

edited by

Richard Lamming
University of Bath

and

Andrew Cox
University of Birmingham

Published by Earlsgate Press.

First Published 1999
Reprinted 2001

British Library Cataloguing in Publication Data.

A catalogue record of this book is available from the British Library.

ISBN 1-873439-81-4

Printed and bound in Great Britain by The Bath Press, Bath

Other Procurement Related Books from Earlsgate Press:

Advanced Supply Management: The Best Practice Debate
by Andrew Cox and Peter Hines (eds). (ISBN 1-873439-51-2)

Business Success by Andrew Cox (ISBN 1-873439-76-8)

Outsourcing: A Business Guide to Risk Management Tools and Techniques by Christopher Lonsdale and Andrew Cox (ISBN 1-873439-61-X).

Innovations in Procurement Management by Andrew Cox (ed) (ISBN 1-873439-46-6)

The European Union at the Crossroads by Paul Furlong and Andrew Cox (eds.) (ISBN 1-873439-16-4)

Public Procurement in the European Community
Series (ISBN 1-873439-30-X)

Volume 1: The Single Market Rules and the Enforcement Regime After 1992 by Andrew Cox (ISBN 1-873439-00-8)

Volume 2: A Guide to the Procurement Cases of the Court of Justice by Sue Arrowsmith (ISBN 1-873439-05-9)

Volume 3: The Texts of the Community Directives by Andrew Cox and Frances Lamont (ISBN 1-873439-40-7)

Volume 4: Remedies for Enforcing the Public Procurement Rules by Sue Arrowsmith (ISBN 1-873439-45-8)

LIST OF CONTRIBUTORS

Gareth Arnold is Project Implementation Manager, Avery Berkel.

Christopher Bouverie-Brine formerly Procurement Planning and Development Manager, London Underground Ltd., now Centre for Strategic Procurement Management, University of Birmingham.

David Court is Director, Government Purchasing Service, Northern Ireland.

Paul Cousins is Lecturer in Purchasing and Operations Management, Centre for Research in Strategic Purchasing and Supply, University of Bath.

Andrew Cox is Professor of Strategic Procurement Management, Centre for Strategic Procurement Management, University of Birmingham.

Peter Hines is Research Fellow, Lean Enterprise Research Centre, Cardiff Business School.

Lyndon Jones is Commercial Manager, Calsonic Llanelli Radiators.

Richard Lamming is CIPS Professor of Purchasing and Supply, Centre for Research in Strategic Purchasing and Supply, University of Bath.

Douglas Macbeth is Professor of Manufacturing Management, University of Glasgow.

David Mannion is the Supplier Development Manager, ICL.

Mark Ralf was Director and Senior Vice President (Purchasing), SmithKline Beecham.

Neil Roberts is Purchasing Manager, Avery Berkel.

Ian Robertson is Managing Director, Land Rover Vehicles.

CONTENTS

INTRODUCTION

PROCUREMENT MANAGEMENT IN THE NEW MILLENNIUM

Andrew Cox and Richard Lamming

This book is a reworking of a book that was conceived in 1993 after a number of discussions between the two editors about what was needed to raise the profile of the purchasing profession in the UK in the 1990s. From our joint discussions it became apparent that there was a need to fuse theory and practice together, in an attempt to raise the level of intellectual and conceptual thinking amongst practitioners and academics working in the field of purchasing and supply management.

That book was entitled Strategic Procurement Management in the 1990s and was the fruit of that praxis. That book was partially funded by the Economic and Social Research Council, who provided us with a research grant to organise two workshops at the Universities of Bath and Birmingham in July 1994. The Chartered Institute of Purchasing and Supply and the DTI also provided support in promoting and launching these two workshops on new concepts in strategic procurement management.

The basic goal of the workshops was to bring practitioners together to discuss the new concepts that leading edge companies were developing as they sought to adopt best practice in their search for added value, lower costs and improved quality. These major new approaches - based on lean supply, partnership and network sourcing, and the use of EDI - can be combined into a general approach which we have labelled strategic procurement management.

In essence this is what that book, and this reworking, are about. How can organisations professionalise their purchasing and supply relationships so that they overcome internal and external constraints which undermine quality, reduce added value and increase cost? It is our contention that this strategic approach is possible and, furthermore, that many companies are already beginning to achieve significant increases in quality and value performance as a result of the adoption of these new concepts and ideas. In order to demonstrate this, and also to help to expand the intellectual environment of debate, we decided to publish the papers from the two workshops in book form. Nothing has caused us to doubt the need to communicate these ideas to practitioners. In this reworking, however, a new first chapter is appended to demonstrate how research into "power and appropriateness" at the CBSP, University of Birmingham, has begun to refocus and challenge some conventional thinking in the area.

This new book is divided into four major sections, each of which represents a major conceptual or practical approach to the transformation of purchasing and supply management. The aim of the initial paper in each section is to provide a theoretical introduction to a particular concept or approach. This is immediately followed by a case study, written by a senior practitioner, explaining how the company under consideration has attempted to introduce the new concept and, whenever possible, to indicate the relative benefits of so doing.

In considering these concepts and cases related to strategic procurement management, lean supply, partnership and network sourcing it is our hope that readers will learn about techniques with which they are unfamiliar. At the same time it is hoped that, if they are themselves actively engaged in developing such concepts practically, either as practitioners or as academics, it might stimulate them to write up their own experiences and ideas and, thereby, contribute to debate and the mutual advancement of the profession. If practitioners would like to take this further they are welcome to contact either of the authors in order to join the International Purchasing and Supply Educational Research Association (IPSERA). This body seeks to bring practitioners and academics together to discuss best practice in purchasing and supply management.

Finally, we should like to thank Shirley Baker and Jackie Potter for helping us organise and run the two original workshops. Also, this new volume would not have been possible without the hard work of Michele Donovan in totally retyping the book and Andy Passey in proof-reading the manuscript.

Andrew Cox and Richard Lamming
March 1999

PART A:

THE STRATEGIC APPROACH TO PROCUREMENT

IMPROVING PROCUREMENT AND SUPPLY COMPETENCE:

On the Appropriate Use of Reactive and Proactive Tools and Techniques in the Public and Private Sectors.*

Andrew Cox

Introduction

In this first chapter a number of key issues are addressed:

i) What an appropriate way of thinking about procurement and supply competence should be, strategically and operationally; how it can be achieved; and, what its possession means for the future role of the purchasing and supply profession.

ii) Why it is that procurement and supply competence cannot be achieved if practitioners continue to remain attached to benchmarking and short-term quick-fix solutions.

iii) Why it is that this way of thinking leads us to conclude that there are likely to be four faces of procurement and supply competence, linked with four ways of thinking about procurement and supply management.

Anyone interested in understanding the thinking that informs the ideas presented in this chapter is recommended to read my recent book: *Business Success*. Some of the ideas discussed here were also presented in a debate held in *Supply Management*, the house journal of the UK's Chartered Institute of Purchasing and Supply (CIPS), in late 1997/early 1998.[1]

The thinking that informed the views on competence expressed by the author in this debate began in the early 1990s during work that was being undertaken at that time, on the regulation of markets and supply chains for the EU. This led to the conclusion that the effective management of supply chains and external resources within companies and national economies was, and is, significantly underdeveloped on a global basis.[2] It was clear then, as it is now, that there is considerable grounds for improvement in procurement and supply competence at all levels of existing public and private sector corporate hierarchies, but not, in my view, necessarily in the way in which many current academics and practitioners appear to believe.

This contrary view needs explaining in some detail. The CIPS in the UK and NAPM in the USA are currently reviewing the whole issue of what the profession should be about. It is clear that there are currently three major views as to what the profession should do to improve its performance and standing in the future. Each of these is discussed in turn below, but it is worth stressing at the outset that, in my view, neither one or the other is *wholly inappropriate* or *wholly appropriate* as the basis for the future restructuring of the profession.

The three views of the future can be defined as follows:

i) *Functional Consolidation*

This view is one that are is held by many traditionalist members of the profession and is focused entirely on the maintenance of the primarily expediting, contract administrative and functional role within which most practitioners have historically operated. Proponents of this viewpoint tend to call for only incremental improvements to the current operational practices that have historically been used, and are quite content with the relative subordinate position of purchasing within the corporate scheme of things. The operational environment within which such people operate is often engineering and/or manufacturing based.

ii) *Functional Imperialism*

Within the profession there is, at more senior levels, a growing group of practitioners who can be defined as functional imperialists. Proponents of this view of the future tend to argue that, because more and more companies are outsourcing major aspects of their spend – especially for support and administrative services – the role of the purchasing manager is becoming more strategic. To those in this school the increasing size of bought-in spend for which they are responsible, and the fact that it has historically been badly managed, ensures that the future of the company's performance and success must now be increasingly the responsibility of purchasing professionals. As a result this school seeks to stake out a claim for the procurement professional to have a position as a functional co-equal on the main board with finance, marketing and operations etc., and to be taken more seriously than in the past. Proponents of this way of thinking can be found in both manufacturing companies that are aggressively outsourcing using core competence thinking, and in the growing number of service based companies that rely on bought-in spend for a substantial share of their ultimate market offering.

iii) The Supply Chain Strategists

It is in this third school, which is made up of a number of academics, who have witnessed the benefits that can flow to innovative practitioners and a growing body of consultancy practices, as well as companies through a more integrated approach to supply chain management, that most of the major innovative ideas for the future of the profession have been derived over the last five years or so. While each of the proponents of this school may have a slightly different spin on what they believe companies should do, my own view is that they tend to share more similarities than dissimilarities. In particular their view of the future of the profession is linked to the idea that the strategic future for purchasing will come from a recognition at senior corporate levels that business success in the future will be based primarily on the competition between supply chains, rather than between individual companies.[3]

This means that the relationships between companies operating within a supply chain become of more importance, and collaboration (in the form of partnerships, networks and associations) takes on greater significance than arms-length purchasing behaviour. Relatedly, there is a focus on Japanese supply chain practice. This is because a significant influence on this way of thinking historically has been the practice of Japanese car manufacturers, and their Western emulators.[4]

The problem for the profession is that the development of these three broad ways of thinking about what the profession should do creates two problems. The first problem is straightforward enough. The bulk of the profession, in background, inclination, training and day-to-day activity, is in *the functional consolidation* camp. Only a small number of senior players in the profession have the opportunity to operate at the more strategically relevant levels, which stimulates the view that a *functional imperialist* approach is possible. Finally, the *supply chain strategists* can command only limited support because the practitioners, consultancies and academics of this persuasion are relatively minuscule in number and, as a result, can only act as agent provocateurs of corporate innovation.

The second problem is even more challenging. As John Ramsay has argued, in response to some of my own arguments, a further difficulty is the fact that the majority of buying is actually undertaken by amateurs.[5] What Ramsay means by this is the fact that, while there are many people who are members of the purchasing and supply profession, they constitute only a small number of those who have professional responsibility – on a day-to-day basis – for buying in public and private sector organisations. These people are, by definition, amateurs who are untrained in the skills and capabilities of effective buying. They are, however, responsible for the bulk of buying that is actually undertaken within organisations. As Ramsay argues correctly, such individuals, from CEOs to secretaries, are untouched by the debates within the profession about what best practice is, or should be. Furthermore, it is unlikely that calls for integrated supply chain management will have much relevance to their day-to-day purchasing activities.

It is not surprising that the profession is, therefore, at a crossroads. There are clearly opportunities out there for the purchasing professional to raise his/her profile, but not everyone can agree on what the most effective way to achieve a more strategic role should be – and some even doubt whether the profession should even try. The problem, however, for those who do want to create a more strategic role is, however, that the opportunities that arise to raise the profession's profile are rarely stimulated by the purchasing professional per se. When opportunities occur they tend to be created by the decisions and actions of other senior colleagues and functions within the corporate hierarchy, not through the purchasing professional being considered automatically as a member of the strategy-making elite within the business.

The difficulty for the profession is, therefore, on two fronts. On the one-hand there is considerable disagreement about whether pursuing a more strategic approach is desirable. Second, and more important, is the problem that, because of these three schools, there is no agreement amongst practitioners or academics about what is the best way to undertake the purchasing and supply activity so that it can be seen to be professional and more effective.

This leaves the profession in an impasse. Over the last five years or so there have been any number of academics jumping on the procurement bandwagon, trying to explain to practitioners that there is a better way to manage purchasing and supply. This has normally involved the view that this should be through a less adversarial and more collaborative approach to relationship management. The practitioner community has either rejected this as nonsense and ignored it; or, embraced it initially with enthusiasm, only to wonder where the ultimate benefit is likely to be after they have adopted this new approach. It is not, in my view, surprising, therefore, that some disgruntled practitioners have sent letters and articles to professional journals arguing that they can do without all these academic fads, that practitioners should concentrate on what they have always done and forget the academics altogether.[6]

Procurement Incompetence: The Problems of Benchmarking and the Quick-Fix Mentality.

One must have some sympathy for this practitioner point of view, even though it can be argued that it is misguided. The reason why it is misguided will become clear later. It is worth stressing here, however, that the reason why practitioners reject many of the recommendations emanating from the existing academic community is because it is guilty of a major error. This major error is the tendency for academics to focus their research activity on *empiricist ways of thinking*. By this phrase one simply means that many academics are guilty of generalising for the business and purchasing community as a whole, on the basis of one or two selective cases drawn from discrete and unique supply chain and market circumstances.

My own view is that this is not the correct way to think about procurement and supply competence. Many academic colleagues do not appear to understand that procurement and supply competence must involve a linkage with the concept of *appropriateness*. They appear to be looking to create what may be termed *a lawyer's brief*: they are seeking evidence to support their already preconceived theories, rather than understanding from first principles what causes business success, and how procurement skills and capabilities (competence) can contribute strategically and operationally to this success. As a result many academic colleagues are led down a cul de sac based on the false and misleading conclusion that, because a particular operational tool or technique is appropriate in one circumstance, it must also be appropriate in all circumstances. This is clearly a logical nonsense because only certain tools and techniques are likely to be appropriate under particular circumstances. To argue that one practice is always appropriate under all circumstances is clearly an affront to common sense.

Unfortunately, while some academic colleagues have been guilty of a false intellectual logic in arguing (or implying) that collaborative and partnership sourcing solutions are the most appropriate under all circumstances, the practitioner community is often just as guilty of false reasoning. Research and practical involvement with industry leads me to conclude that there is considerable evidence that practitioners also do not understand the appropriateness of particular interventions under specific contingent supply chain and market circumstances. While there are many practitioners who have developed operational rules of thumb that allow them to understand when certain things are appropriate, it is true to say that there is no evidence within the practitioner or consulting communities (that I am are aware of) of any individual or company having properly codified the full range of tools and techniques that are available to purchasing professionals, and the appropriate way in which these should be used in specific contingent circumstances. What does appear to exist in the practitioner and consulting community is, however, an operational methodology based on quick-fix solutions and benchmarking thinking.

Many practitioners may wonder what is wrong with a quick-fix based on benchmarking the practices of other practitioners? On the face of it, if someone else has found a better way of doing what it is that you are currently doing, then surely there can be no error in copying and adapting the practices of others? At one level, the answer to this question must be a categorical no. Clearly, if someone does know how to do something, and they are prepared to allow (or unable to stop) other practitioners from copying them, it is obvious that this is a short-cut, quick-fix for business success.

At another level it is my view that this benchmarking way of thinking leads to fads that fail because people do not understand the appropriateness of particular practices for specific companies under discrete and unique circumstances.[7] Obviously, if the benchmarking activity is simply the copying and adaptation of what others are doing in essentially similar non-critical and administrative support areas of the business, then the case for copying as a short-cut may be less problematic than if the practice is adopted in relation to understanding how a company achieves a competitive advantage against other companies in a particular supply chain or market.

The major problem with benchmarking is that it leads to intellectual incompetence at a general level within a business, and to procurement incompetence at the strategic level. This is because business success comes from the ability to understand what are the ultimate reasons why a company is able to appropriate value for itself through its activities within a particular supply chain and market. Only by knowing why a company has been able to improve quality or reduce costs, for a particular product or service in a particular circumstance, is it possible for a practitioner to develop the competence to know what it is that they should focus their effort on when it comes to competitive resource management.

My view is that much of the problem with the purchasing and supply profession results from its relative inability to understand how to think appropriately about business success, through its over attachment to benchmarking and copying behaviour. Unless practitioners are able to understand, from first principles, what it is that engenders business success then it is impossible for them to be able to know what it is that they should be doing to improve performance, either operationally or strategically, for the specific business for which they work.

This is not just a semantic point. It goes to the very heart of the problem facing the profession, both in knowing what it should do to be competent operationally, and in knowing what it should do to impact the strategic corporate agenda in the future. If the profession does not understand which interventions are critical to business success, and under what circumstances, then it will never be able to impact the strategic agenda and will always be reacting to the strategic decisions of others. The benchmarking mentality that bedevils the profession will, therefore, consign those who adopt it to a functional and reactive role forever.

So what is to be done? My own view is that the profession should seek *procurement and supply competence* if it wishes to develop a significant role within any public or private sector organisation. The reason for this is that procurement and supply competence is not necessarily well understood either at the operational or at the strategic levels in the business.[8] By developing this competence, then, it may be possible for some (but certainly not all) practitioners to educate more senior players in the business to the importance of this capability. Although the space is not available here to fully explain what this means in practice, in the section that follows the basis of what I believe procurement and supply competence to be is outlined.

Procurement and Supply Competence: On Power and the Selection of Appropriate Tools and Techniques for the Effective Leverage of Supply Chain Resources and Assets.

It can be argued that the route to strategic and operational alignment, for those responsible for the management of external resources in a business, is through the development of procurement and supply competence. Procurement and supply competence is based, not on the benchmarking, or slavish copying, of the practices of Japanese or any other companies, but on the development of an understanding of what creates success for any and all businesses. It requires, therefore, that practitioners begin *to think* about the nature of business success in all its contingent circumstances.

In my view business success for private sector organisations always requires two, although sometimes three, major competencies:

- *The first competence that is necessary is a marketing and sales ability.* Without the ability to manage demand effectively, and to sell that which has been produced, it is unlikely that anyone could make money.

- *The second competence is a procurement and supply ability.* This is the capability to be able to procure (by ownership and/or control) those resources that will allow the company to appropriate and accumulate value (profits) for itself from the utilisation of the marketing and selling competence.

- *The third competence that is often (although not always) required is the transformation competence.* This is the ability to change inputs into more valuable outputs within the boundary of the firm.

Clearly, many companies require this latter transformation capability, which is why operations and engineering are so important at strategic levels in companies. It is also true, however, that it is possible to make money without transforming anything: one can do it merely by buying and selling. It follows, therefore, that an entrepreneurial approach to business ought to focus, first, on the ability to market and sell that which can be procured. Transformation is only really necessary under some, not all, circumstances. These first two (or primary) competencies are, however, required for all companies, under all circumstances.

Given the strategic importance of the ability to buy (procure) supply chain resources for any business it comes as something of a surprise, therefore, to discover that most companies do not hold this capability in very high regard. The reason is self-evident. It is clearly because the dominant way of thinking in the last two hundred years has been based on the idea that vertical integration and internal control of key resources, and their manufacturing transformation of inputs, is the best way to make money. This view of the world is also linked to a particular view of the structure of power within supply chains, and the hierarchy of power within organisations. It is a view that holds that companies should only buy externally non-critical commodities and support services. It is a way of thinking that effectively consigns the purchasing function to a reactive, order processing and transactional contracting role.

But is it, as some would argue, a wholly inappropriate way of thinking about what the purchasing role should be? In my view, it is neither a wholly inappropriate or wholly appropriate way of thinking about procurement and supply competence. Under certain circumstances it can be argued that it may well be the most appropriate thing to do. This would be so if the balance of forces within a particular supply chain are so aligned that the effective procurement role internally should be with the engineering specifier, and the transactional competence can be left to a clerical and administrative contract management purchasing function. Under other circumstances the balance of power within the supply chain may make such an arrangement wholly inappropriate. The key is to know when it is and when it is not. This is procurement and supply competence.

The focus here on the concept of power is of critical importance to our understanding of procurement and supply competence. To understand business success it is, in my view, essential that practitioners and academics understand that business is about the effective management of power. It is not, in my view, about working collaboratively, or on a basis of trust. How one deals with others (unkindly or generously) cannot be an end in itself in business, it can only ever, be a means to an end. The end must always be the same: to make money by closing markets to other possible competitors by the most effective management of supply chain resources.

If we accept this way of thinking about business success it is clear that understanding what should be insourced within a company (and why), and what can be safely outsourced (and how), must be a key strategic competence for any company – and for any public agency. It is interesting to note, however, that most purchasing practitioners have very little direct and proactive involvement in the key make/buy decisions made by their organisations. Ironically, based on current research, it would appear that those that do make such decisions at a strategic level do not appear to have developed robust methodologies to allow them to undertake effective make/buy decision-making.[9]

Herein, surely, lies the key to that elevated role which some individuals within the profession seek for themselves? If individuals within the profession could, through their ability to understand procurement and supply competence, develop a robust theoretical and conceptual methodology to assist any, and all, organisations to undertake their *'boundary of the firm'* decisions, and the subsequent management of external resources more appropriately, then both a strategically and operationally aligned impact would be assured. This might not ensure that everyone in the profession would have a strategic role, but that those who have the aptitude to rise would do so with the appropriate skills and capabilities. To be able to develop such an impact it is essential, however, that we know not only where the effective boundary of the firm should be, and how internal and external and resources should be managed, but how this can be undertaken effectively under *all contingent circumstances*, not just some of them.

This is the crux of the problem facing the profession's aspiration for strategic elevation. There is a need for everyone in the business community, not just for purchasing professionals, to understand what procurement and supply competence means in theory and practice, and how it can contribute to sustained business success. My own view is that procurement and supply competence for purchasing professionals (and for all other business practitioners) must start from the recognition of the four dimensions of supply.[10] Understanding what are the four dimensions of supply involves an ability to differentiate between:

- **The ability to find more professional, but still essentially reactive, ways of purchasing what is currently offered within an existing supply market *(The First Dimension of Supply)*.**

- **The capacity to realign current supply chain relationships to create innovative and waste reducing ways of delivering existing products and services *(The Second Dimension of Supply).***

- **The ability to analyse and understand the structure of power and leverage that operates within existing supply chains *(The Third Dimension of Supply)*.**

- **The ability to understand the functionality that flows through supply chains, which must be fundamentally transformed to destroy existing supply chain power to create new supply chain power structures (*The Fourth Dimension of Supply*).**

By understanding these four ways of thinking about the nature of supply it becomes clear that most of the purchasing profession (academics and practitioners alike) are only really operating at the first and second dimensions of supply. To develop procurement and supply competence, and for the profession to have the strategic impact it desires, it is necessary for practitioners to operate at all four levels of understanding. This is because business success is ultimately about understanding the conditions under which individuals or companies can obtain ownership or control of supply chain resources, which they can effectively leverage against suppliers, competitors, customers (and employees), in order that they and their shareholders can appropriate and accumulate value for themselves. Business success is not, therefore, ultimately, about passing value to customers (whatever marketing people and the proponents of the *supply chain strategy* school may say) it is about keeping it for one self.

It seems clear that an improvement in the role of the profession in the business community will not come from the adoption of any one of the three schools of thought discussed earlier. The reason for this is obvious. It is because each of the three schools outlined – the *functional consolidators*, the *functional imperialists* and the *supply chain strategists* – is right and wrong at the same time. The problem is, in my view, that each of the three ways of thinking about procurement and supply competence can be correct under certain circumstances; but equally each way of thinking is incorrect under other circumstances. The problem is that none of the three schools appears to know under what circumstances their approach is the appropriate thing for a practitioner to do, and when it is not.

Figure 1.1 Procurement and Supply Competence

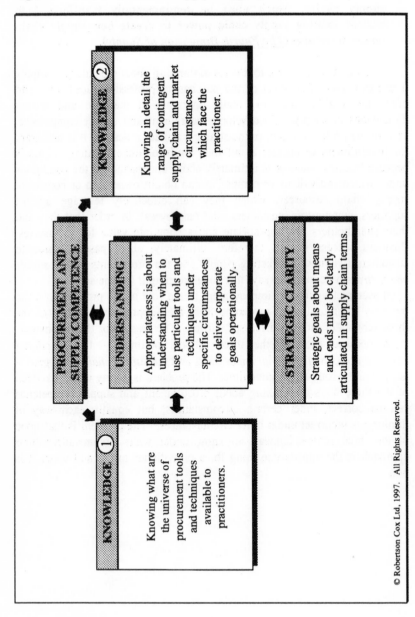

The only correct way of thinking about procurement and supply competence is surely for practitioners to be taught to recognise, from first principles, that a properly grounded understanding of what cause business success is their surest route to significant strategic and operational influence in the business. Such an approach would lead them to recognise, as Figure 1.1 demonstrates, that procurement and supply competence ultimately flows from knowing three things:

- First, practitioners must know what the full range of *tools and techniques* available for practitioners to use to achieve effective leverage over supply chain resources is. My view is that this will lead them to recognise the importance of *critical supply chain assets* – or the most important resources within particular supply chains, that allow them to appropriate value.

- Second, practitioners will understand the significance of the *contingent circumstances* that confront them. By this I mean that tools and techniques are one thing, but they must be applied within particular circumstances. In my view the circumstances that they must be used within will always be within specific supply chains, that have unique structural properties that over-determine which tools and techniques will be the most effective to achieve leverage (value appropriation and accumulation).

- Finally, practitioners who have procurement and supply competence will also possess a knowledge and understanding of *appropriateness*. By appropriateness I mean the ability to know when it makes sense to adopt one tool or technique for effective leverage within the specific contingent circumstances that face them. It is clear that this is only possible, however, if practitioners have a clear knowledge of the strategic vision (means and ends) that informs the value appropriation and accumulation strategy of the company.

This leads to an interesting conclusion. This is that the future of the profession will be enhanced if practitioners and academics can begin to understand the need for appropriateness in business relationships. This is the key to procurement and supply competence. Some ways of thinking appropriately are described below. These are important because, in reading through the concepts and cases in this volume, it will be necessary for the reader to understand what the concept is, how it has been applied within a specific corporate context and, most importantly of all, whether copying or adapting it is, in fact, an appropriate thing to do. This is the real test of competence: not just knowing that something can be done but understanding whether it is sensible to try to do it in one's own circumstances. An understanding of what this means for the choices practitioners have when they seek to choose between collaborative or more adversarial relationships is presented in summary in the next section.

Recognising Appropriateness in Procurement and Supply Relationships.

1. The False Dichotomy of Adversarialism and Collaboration.

If practitioners and academics accept this way of thinking about appropriateness under specific contingent circumstances they may begin to understand that the distinction that is often made between adversarial and collaborative relationship management is misguided. It can be argued that the choice of appropriate business relationships is never between being adversarial or collaborative. In reality all business relationships are potentially adversarial, and if this is the case then collaboration is a means to and end, not an end in itself. Those who have followed the argument so far will be able to understand perfectly, therefore, why:

"Collaboration is a form of leverage by other means".

It follows that, if collaboration is not an end in itself in business relationships, then it must be a means to an end. While there is no doubt that collaboration with other organisations can be an appropriate thing to do under specific circumstances, is it clear under which circumstances collaboration is the appropriate thing to do, and when it is not? Knowing the answer to this question is arguably one of the key abilities that a person who has procurement and supply competence should be able to

Figure 1.2: The Four Principles of Effective Leverage

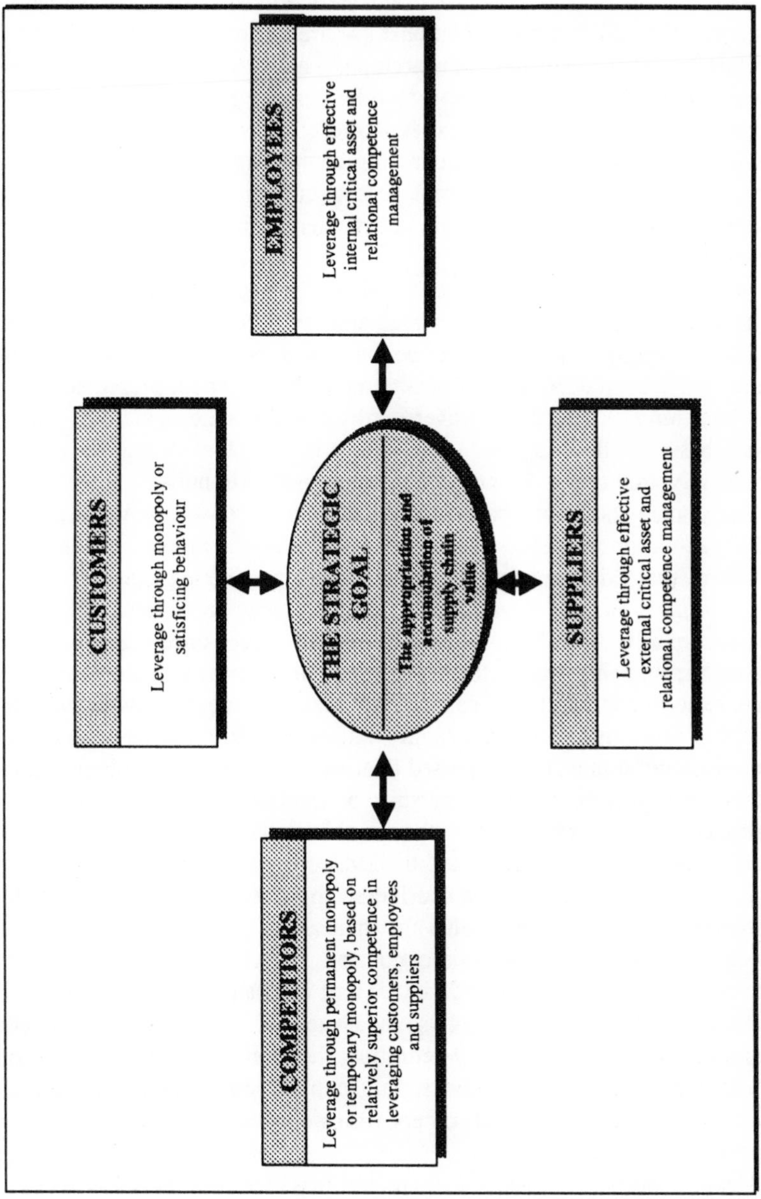

EMPLOYEES
Leverage through effective internal critical asset and relational competence management

CUSTOMERS
Leverage through monopoly or satisficing behaviour

THE STRATEGIC GOAL
The appropriation and accumulation of supply chain value

SUPPLIERS
Leverage through effective external critical asset and relational competence management

COMPETITORS
Leverage through permanent monopoly or temporary monopoly, based on relatively superior competence in leveraging customers, employees and suppliers

Adapted from Andrew Cox, Business Success (Earlsgate Press, 1997 p.189) demonstrate. It can be argued that anyone who has this ability will also recognise that all business relationships are, ultimately, based on the adversarial pursuit of value appropriation. This conflict obviously occurs between direct competitors trying to offer similar products and services within a supply chain. It also exists, however, between the customer and the selling company; between the buying company and its suppliers; and, between the owners and the employees within any organisation. This understanding, described in Figure 1.2, is referred to as *the four principles of effective leverage.*[11]

It has been argued that to take this view is to argue that adversarialism is the goal that business should pursue and, by implication, that this is to preach an ideology that should not be the goal of business practice.[12] This is clearly a fundamental misunderstanding of the argument presented here. It is one thing to argue that adversarialism is the state of nature within which business does operate, and altogether another thing to argue, normatively, that this is the end which business should pursue. Since there is clearly some confusion about what the difference between adversarialism and collaboration in business relationships is, a brief summary of the false dichotomy that exists in some current procurement thinking is necessary.

In *Business Success* it was argued that the human condition is to live in a state of relative and absolute scarcity. Furthermore, since what is scarce is what human beings value, then it follows that material success must have some relationship with the capacity to make scarce the ownership or control of those things that are highly valued by many people. Following from this logic it must be recognised that, by definition, those things which are capable of scarcity in ownership or control cannot be owned or controlled by everyone, since if they could be they would no longer be scarce in ownership or control, and their value would diminish accordingly. In order to be successful in business, therefore, companies seek to appropriate and accumulate value for themselves through making highly valued things scarce in ownership or control. This means that the objective state of nature within which individuals and companies exist materially is one in which they must seek to close the ownership and control of valuable (scarce) resources to others. By definition, therefore, *the objective state of nature* under capitalism is adversarialism by owners and controllers of material resources vis-à-vis all others who would seek to wrest control or ownership from them.[13]

Under conditions of scarcity, therefore, it is clear that *business success (under all circumstances) involves the pursuit of self-interest.* To say this is not, however, to argue that collaboration is an inappropriate thing to do operationally. On the contrary, it is clear that, while selfishness is the basis on which all business relationships objectively operate (for even supply chain versus supply chain competition operates on this selfish basis does it not?), there will be contingent circumstances under which co-operating with others will be the best means to achieve an intended goal. In some circumstances, however, collaboration with others will clearly be the most inappropriate thing to do.

The key requirement for practitioners, therefore, is to recognise when it is appropriate for them to collaborate to achieve an intended goal and when it is not. Key questions practitioners must ask, therefore, when they consider collaboration with horizontal or vertical partners, are:

- *What are the motives of those with whom we might collaborate?*
- *What are the grounds for opportunism and self-seeking behaviour on our collaborators part if we work closely with them?*
- *What are the risks to our ownership and control of the critical assets from which we appropriate and accumulate value?*
- *Is there a proper coincidence of interest that will allow us to collaborate successfully in the short and long-terms?*

What should be clear from this simple statement of the conditions for effective collaboration is that the key for practitioners is not knowing that collaboration can lead to business success – clearly it can – but to know under what circumstances success is likely to occur, and when it is not. To know that collaboration is a way of undertaking business relationships is not the same as saying that it can always be made to work effectively, or that it is always the best way to undertake business to business interaction. Anyone arguing this way really would be guilty of imposing an ideological view of the world on reality. It is, however, a way of thinking to which some practitioners and some academic colleagues have become dangerously attached in recent years.

More worrying perhaps is the fact that to argue this way, and to claim that business practitioners should give up adversarialism in favour of collaboration is to be guilty of the creation of a false dichotomy. This false dichotomy is the mistaken view that the opposite of adversarialism is collaboration. A moment's reflection will demonstrate that this is a mistaken view. The opposite of adversarial is non-adversarial. The opposite of collaboration is arms-length. It seems clear, therefore, that many practitioners and academics may be guilty of a simple error of typological categorisation. Many practitioners and academics appear to believe that to collaborate is to be non-adversarial. Clearly, whether or not one should use collaboration in a non-adversarial way depends on the circumstance. Sometimes one may collaborate to achieve an adversarial end (using guile and stealth), or one may use collaboration without any ulterior motive whatsoever. If this is true then to argue that collaboration is always non-adversarial is, as Figure 1.3 demonstrates, to be guilty of seriously underestimating the range of contingent circumstances that can face the practitioner. Practitioners can choose to use collaboration while pursuing adversarial relationships, or they can choose arms-length relationships. Similarly, arms-length or collaboration are both alternative ways of managing non-adversarial relationships.

2. When is Supply Chain Integration Appropriate?

Linked to this criticism of the claim that collaboration is the most appropriate way for practitioners to manage in all business circumstances must be a rebuttal of the view that supply chain integration is also the most appropriate thing to do for business success. The importance of managing an integrated supply chain has been recognised in *Business Success*, and referred to throughout that work as *the second dimension of supply*.[14] Despite this some critics have argued that because some companies have used collaboration and supply chain integration successfully – for example unspecified companies in the North Sea, BHS, Somerfield, the Lane Group, Wal-Mart and General Foods – collaboration and integration *must* be the most effective way to manage business relationships.[15]

Unfortunately, to argue this way is to fail to recognise the importance of the concept of appropriateness. The fact that some companies have achieved short-term business improvement through working more closely with some suppliers is hardly a refutation of the central argument that there are many different ways in which companies can manage relationships in order to achieve competitive advantage. What is crucial for any company in a supply chain relationship is not the fact that a collaborative form of relationship exists but whether or not they have achieved a sustainable competitive advantage (i.e. relative monopoly position based on superior competence) when compared with their direct competitors in the chain.

Figure 1.3: The False Dichotomy of Adversarial and Collaboration

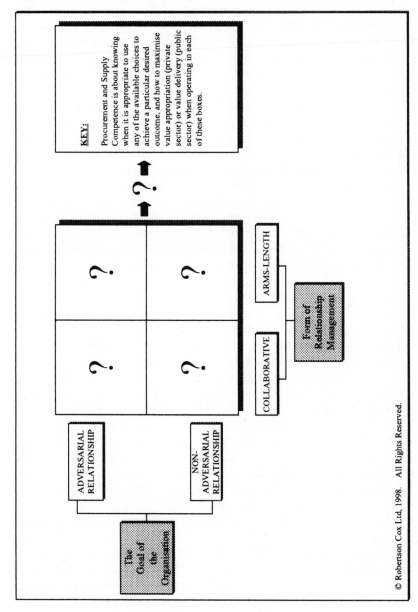

Let us assume, for the sake of argument, that each of the retail companies indicated above that have achieved logistical success has done so by working closely with their suppliers. Let us also further assume that each of the suppliers in the chain to the end retailer has now achieved competitive advantage over its direct competitors. What is the motive of that supplier likely to be? Will it be to try to sell the same service to all other potential players in all of the similar types of supply chain that require the service it now monopolises, or will it be to keep it for the original customer that it worked to develop it with? My guess is (in the West at least) that the relatively superior supplier will have every incentive to pass the innovation to other customers in order to grow their own business. This means then that, unless the retailer in the chain has some mechanism by which it can control innovation and own it in a monopolistic way, what it has created will be passed to every one of its direct competitors. Thus, the empirical evidence that short-term gains can be made by collaboration does not refute the basic argument that it is only if an innovation can be owned and controlled effectively (i.e. as a relative monopolist in a selfish way) that business success can be sustained over the long-term.

Despite this there are clearly major business benefits that can be obtained from the ability to know when it is possible to control and to integrate supply chains so as to compete more aggressively and effectively against other supply chains. One point is worth making however – although the space here does not permit an in-depth elaboration. Most of those who argue the case for supply chain versus supply chain integration seem to have scant understanding of the immense difficulty of operationalising this way of working effectively. Creating a totally integrated and collaborative approach in the absence of a major critical asset owner, who is capable of acting as the impresario of the total supply chain, is clearly likely to be highly problematic. In the absence of the conditions that generate and sustain such a total supply chain impresario, it is probable that the benefits of supply chain integration (and of supply chain versus supply chain competition) are likely to be stillborn.

It is, therefore, irresponsible of consultants and academics to encourage practitioners to seek supply chain integration if they neither understand the structural properties of supply chains, nor how to achieve the necessary power to achieve supply chain integration. This is particularly true when it is clear that many of those recommending supply chain integration appear to be unaware of the major risks they may be running in recommending virtual integration of supply chains.[16] One of the key risks that my own research has revealed is the loss of critical assets and activities to suppliers by short-sighted practitioners, pursuing the latest business fads.[17] If this is occurring through the lemming-like rush by practitioners to outsource all non-core activities, it can only be happening because many practitioners do not fully understand when it is appropriate to outsource, or when it is possible to virtually integrate a supply chain. The fact that some companies have achieved this, and have been successful in business, is clearly not an indication that to do so will inevitably lead to success for others.

Competence and the Four Faces of Procurement and Supply Management.

How then can anyone know what is the appropriate thing to do under any specific circumstance? This is clearly a difficult question to resolve as the discussion above about the problematic nature of understanding appropriateness, and being able to generalise from specific cases, demonstrates. This question is, however, made even more difficult when practitioners address the question from very different operating environments. Perhaps the most obvious distinction that is often made is that between the public and private sectors. Is what is done in the private sector always the most appropriate thing for those in the public sector to do, and vice versa? Clearly the answer will be sometimes yes – when both are in the same circumstance – and sometimes no – when they are not. The problem is compounded, however, because sometimes we should be proactive and sometimes reactive when operating with suppliers in either the public or private sectors. So what is to be done?

Perhaps the best way to address this question is not to think first about the public or private sectors but to ask the question: what is the difference between the *professionalisation of the purchasing and supply function* within an organisation and the development of *procurement and supply competence*? By answering this question it will become possible to understand the four strategic and operational faces of supply and procurement competence, and provide some pointers as to when it is appropriate for practitioners to adopt each one of these ways of operating under specific contingent circumstances.

It is important, at the outset of this discussion of appropriateness in strategic and operational alignment, to define what is meant by each of the two types of organisational focus and capability. By *purchasing and supply functional professionalism* is meant that process by which corporate decision-makers recognise the need to improve their existing structures and processes, as well as practitioner skills and capabilities, within the purchasing and supply function in their company. This recognition normally involves a reappraisal of the purchasing function in relation to existing in-house functions (in particular the existing manufacturing and production function). This may involve a reappraisal of current make/buy strategies and a repositioning of the purchasing and supply function within the corporate hierarchy, with an increasing focus on ways to improve the internal cost structure behind the delivery of the function.

Relatedly, this reappraisal can lead to a new commercial role and responsibility for purchasing and supply management. Instead of its historic role as a reactive and administrative function purchasing can become more proactively involved in internal and external supply chain management. This process normally involves the function developing a more proactive approach to supplier appraisal, development and performance. This new approach normally involves a rejection of price offerings from suppliers in favour of a focus on the total costs of ownership, and the development of a more sophisticated understanding of the range of supply relationships that are available to achieve long-term value for money. This may also involve an emphasis on the total integration and management of the existing logistics and supply chain, as the basis for waste reduction and operational efficiency throughout the corporate supply chain for current products and services.

The professional approach to purchasing and supply functionalism described above can still be seen, however, as primarily reactive in conception. While there is little doubt that a reappraisal of the purchasing and supply function, and the interventions that are necessary to achieve this, require a more proactive and innovative approach by purchasing professionals, this approach is still primarily located within an operational effectiveness way of thinking about competitive advantage. The reason for this is because the modus operandi of this approach is based on two distinct, but linked, views of how to achieve operational effectiveness for existing products and services. The first goal is the desire to improve the internal alignment of the current purchasing function with other operational silos within the company by redefining roles and responsibilities. The second aspect is a linked attempt to deliver current products and services in a more operationally efficient way through a more professional approach to existing logistics and supply chain processes and relationships.

As effective as this may be in improving the current operational effectiveness of the way in which products and services are delivered it can be argued that this innovation is still within the existing product and service delivery paradigm. The company is still trying to find a more effective way of delivering existing products and services. This is a relatively reactive way of thinking about corporate success when it is compared with a truly proactive approach that focuses on how a company can realign the structure of power within current supply chains in order to create competitive advantage. Such an approach would focus on how completely new products and services can be created in order to deliver the same supply chain functionality to customers, but in a superior way, which competitors would find difficult to imitate.

This way of thinking about the effective management and leverage of supply chain resources has been discussed elsewhere.[19] Without discussing these ideas in detail here it is clear, however, that sustained competitive advantage in the long-term requires that companies must do more than simply innovate with the internal and external delivery of existing products and services. Clearly, sustained competitive advantage requires that companies *also* focus on how to create new products and services in the primary supply chains within which they are involved.

This proactive and innovative way of thinking about supply chain power and functionality requires more than just a focus on purchasing and supply professionalism, it requires an understanding of effective resource leverage and procurement competence throughout a company. The reason for this resides in the fact that product and service innovation is almost always a supply chain phenomenon. This means that an understanding of the importance of supply innovation and control is an essential requirement for the effective management of corporate strategy and operational practice in well run businesses. This way of thinking about corporate strategy and operational practice is referred to here as *procurement and supply competence.*

All organisations, whether they are in the public or private sectors, therefore, have to be able to come to terms with the need to focus simultaneously on *static efficiency* through cost reduction and purchasing and supply functional professionalism, and *dynamic efficiency* through supply alignment and procurement competence. These four faces of competence are outlined in Figure 4.1.

Figure 1.4: The Four Faces of Procurement and Supply Competence

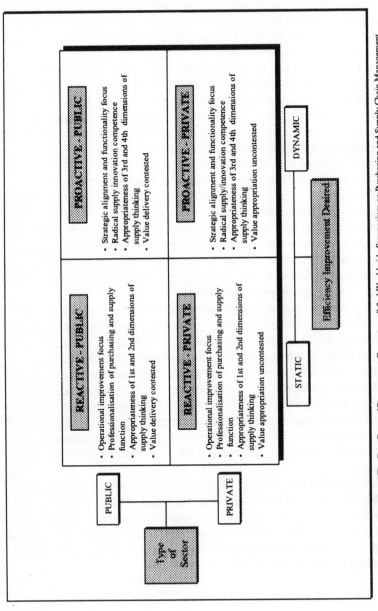

Adapted from Andrew Cox. "The Four Faces of Procurement Competence" 2nd Worldwide Symposium on Purchasing and Supply Chain Management (London:CIPS/NAPM/IPSERA, 1st April 1998)

3. *What is to be Done? Procurement and Supply Competence and the Problem of Appropriateness*

It is one thing to know that there may be reactive and proactive ways of managing procurement and supply, and that what needs to be done in the public and private sectors may also differ, but how does a practitioner know what they should do in any of these four types of circumstance?

As Figure 1.1 indicated earlier, it is clear that for anyone to achieve *procurement and supply competence* an understanding of appropriateness must be achieved. This can only be developed if four things are internalised by practitioners. First, there must be a proper knowledge of the full range of reactive and proactive tools and techniques (like make/buy, purchasing portfolio management, supplier positioning, strategic source planning, margin cost analysis, contract methodologies, negotiation, relational competence and congruence analysis and logistical techniques, etc.) that are available to *anyone* involved in business when they make decisions about the effective ownership and control of supply chain assets. Second, there must be a proper knowledge of the contingent supply chain and market circumstances within which a company is operating. Both of these types of knowledge – termed Knowledge 1 and 2 in the Figure – are absolutely essential for procurement and business competence to be achieved. It is my view, however, that most practitioners have only some grasp of Knowledge 1 and almost no grasp of Knowledge 2.

Furthermore, it can be argued that many academic colleagues argue for particular approaches (tools and techniques) under Knowledge 1, without a proper grasp of the contingent circumstances within which these tools are to be implemented. It is my view, therefore, that practitioners, consultants and academics should not recommend tools and techniques unless they have a proper understanding of the likely impact of the use of those tools or techniques in a particular contingent circumstance. It follows, of course, that no amount of refining of the currently available tools and techniques will be of any use unless academics and practitioners begin to understand in more detail the contingent circumstances that face them.

It is clear from research interviews that many practitioners do not analyse in detail the specific supply chain and market circumstances within which they operate and, consequently, it is hardly surprising that they do not know what is the appropriate course of action. For any practitioner to know what to do, therefore, requires not only a far better understanding of the properties of the supply chains within which they operate, but also a better understanding of what are the appropriate tools and techniques to use under all and any contingent circumstances. This cannot be achieved for any practitioner in the absence of a guiding theory about what causes business success in any, and all, circumstances. Such a theory should be capable of describing and predicting that which is likely to be the most appropriate thing to do under all circumstances.

This is the challenge that will face practitioners as they read through this volume. They will need to know when it is appropriate for them to develop and adapt any of the approaches outlined in what follows. When is Partnership Sourcing an appropriate thing to do? Is Lean Supply something that should be adopted? Will EDI help my business or hinder it? It will not be clear to practitioners as they read about these concepts which ones are likely to be beneficial or harmful to them. So how will they choose successfully? My own view is that they can only choose successfully if they have a real understanding of what business is about from first principles, and know how to operationalise this in the unique supply chain and market circumstances that face them. If practitioners do not understand this then they will have no hope of choosing wisely from amongst the variety of tools and techniques currently on offer to them.

This dilemma can be briefly illuminated by reference to a concept (tool or technique) that I recently devised to assist practitioners. It is called Relational Competence and Congruence Analysis. The tool is outlined in Figure 1.5. It basically asks practitioners to locate their current suppliers along two matrices, based on the current relational competence (high/low) and current relational congruence (high/low). It is clear that the ideal situation for buying companies is to have their suppliers in the top right hand box (Compatibility). But when using this tool with practitioners it has become clear to me that the majority believe that, in the absence of the ideally compatible supplier, it is always best to choose suppliers in the top left hand (Congruence Improvement) box. What does this tell me about the thinking of most practitioners? It tells me that they make judgements on the basis of a limited understanding of the circumstances that are appropriate for the use of particular tools and techniques.

Space does not allow for a full development of the ways in which this tool might be used reactively *and* proactively. Suffice it to say, however, that the real task for practitioners is to understand when, *and how*, a particular tool might be used with benefit to their organisation. It is not enough simply to know that a tool or technique exists (although we must surely know about particular tools and techniques before one can implement them), the real test of competence is to both know when and how a tool or technique can be used for benefit, and also when it is a waste

Figure 1.5: Relational Competence and Congruence Analysis

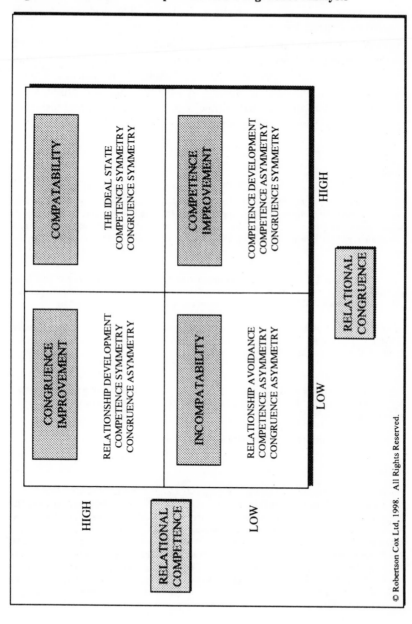

of effort to try.   My own experience in public and private sector
organisations leads me to conclude, however, that knowing what is
appropriate in procurement and supply is not something that is, as yet, well
developed amongst strategic or operational practitioners. It is to be hoped
that the concepts and cases in this volume will allow practitioners to better
understand the range of tools and techniques available (Knowledge 1) and,
by thinking about the cases in which they have been operationalised, when
they may be appropriately used (Knowledge 2). If it fulfils this task then
this volume will have served its purpose.

Notes

*This article is based on a paper that was first presented by the author under the title: "The Four
Faces of Procurement Competence: Managing Dynamic and Static Efficiency in Public and Private
Sector Supply" in the proceedings of *2nd Woldwide Symposium on Purchasing and Supply
Chain Management* held by the CIPS/NAPM/IPSERA in London at the Forum Hotel on 1-3
April, 1998).

[1] The debate in the UK over the issues raised in Andrew Cox, *Business Success: A Way of
Thinking about Strategy, Critical Supply Chain Assets and Operational Best Practice* (Boston,
UK: Earlsgate Press, 1997, www.earlsgatepress.com) took place in the following articles:

Andrew Cox, "On Power, Appropriateness and Procurement Competence", *Supply Management*,
(24th October 1997), pp.24-27; "Right to Reply", *Supply Management*, (27th November 1997),
pp.24-29; and, Andrew Cox, " Clarifying Complexity", *Supply Management*, (29th January 1998),
pp.34-36.

Issues raised by the debate are also taken up in Andrew Cox and Peter Hines (eds.), *Advanced
Supply Management: The Best Practice Debate* (Boston, UK: Earlsgate Press, 1997,
www.earlsgatepress.com).

[2] The work referred to here was published in the following books and articles:

Books:

Paul Furlong and Andrew Cox (eds.), *The European Union at the Crossroads: Problems in
Implementing the Single Market Project* (Boston, UK: Earlsgate Press, 1995); Andrew Cox, Paul
Furlong and Pat Coleman, *The European Procurement Directory, Volumes 1-3* (Boston, UK:
Earlsgate Press, 1995), Andrew Cox, Paul Furlong and Pat Coleman, *The European Utilities
Procurement Directory* (Boston, UK: Earlsgate Press, 1995); Keith Hartley and Andrew Cox,
The Costs of Non-Europe in Defence Procurement (Brussels: European Commission, DGIII,
1993); Andrew Cox, *Public Procurement in the European Community: Volume 1: The Single
Market Rules and the Enforcement Regime* (Boston, UK: Earlsgate Press, 1993); and, Andrew
Cox and Paul Furlong, *A Modern Companion to the European Community*, (Cheltenham:
Edward Elgar, 1991).

Articles:

David Mayes, Keith Hartley and Andrew Cox, "The Impact of the Rules", in D.G. Mayes (ed), *The Evolution of the Single European Market* (Cheltenham: Edward Elgar, 1997), pp.87-113; Keith Hartley, Stephen Martin and Andrew Cox, "Public Purchasing in the European Union: Some Evidence from Contract Awards", *The International Journal of Public Sector Management*, Vol.10, Nos. 4/5 (1997), pp.279-293; Andrew Cox and Paul Furlong, "Cross Border Trade and Cross Border Contract Awards: The Intellectual Myopia at the Heart of the EU Procurement Rules", *European Journal of Purchasing and Supply Management* (1997), Vol.3, No.1, pp.9-10; Andrew Cox and Paul furlong, "The Jury is Still Out for Utilities Procurement", *Public Procurement Law Review*, (1996), No.3, pop.56-67; Andrew Cox and Paul Furlong, "The Impact of the Public Procurement Directives on EU Contract Awards in 1993" in D.G. Mayes (ed), *The Evolution of the Rules for a Single European Market, Part II: Rules, Democracy and the Environment* (Brussels, European Commission, Cost A7, Vol.4, 1995), pp.115-142; Andrew Cox and Paul Furlong, "Utilities Procurement and the EU Procurement Rules", *Utilities Policy,* (July/October 1995) Vol.5, no.3/4), pp.199-206; Andrew Cox and Paul Furlong, "European Procurement Rules and National Preference", *Journal of Construction Procurement*, (1995) Vol.1, No.2, pp.87-99; Andrew Cox, "Market Entry and Non-National Suppliers", *European Journal of Purchasing and Supply Management,* (194), Vol.1, No.4,pp.1-9; Andrew Cox and Joe Sanderson, "From the Mobilisation of Bias to Trade Wars", *European Journal of Public Policy* (Autumn 1994) Vol.1, No.2, pp.263-282; Andrew Cox, "Derogation, Subsidiarity and the Single Market", *Journal of Common Market Studies* (June 1994), Vol.32, No.2, pp.127-147; Paul Furlong, Frances Lamont and Andrew Cox, "Competition or Partnership: CCT and EC Public Procurement Rules in the Single Market", *European Journal of Purchasing and Supply Management* (March 1994), Vol.1, No.1, pp.37-43; Andrew Cox, "The Future of European Defence Policy: The Case for a Centralised Defence Procurement Agency", *Public Procurement Law Review*, (1993), Vol.3, No.2, pp.65-86; Andrew Cox, "Public Procurement in the European Community; Is a Fully Integrated Market Achievable?", *Public Money and Management* (July-September 1993), pp.29-35; and, Andrew Cox, "Implementing the 1992 Public Procurement Policy: Public and Private Obstacles to the Creation of the Single European Market", *Public Procurement Policy Review,* (1992) Vol.1, No.2, pp. 139-154.

[3] There is an immense literature on the issue of supply chain integration and the benefits of partnerships and networks in supply management. Some of the key recent texts include:

Martin Christopher, *Marketing Logistics* (Oxford: Butterworth-Heinemann, 1997); Peter Hines, *Creating World Class Suppliers* (London: Pitman, 1994); Richard Lamming, *Beyond Partnership,* (New York: Prentice Hall, 1993); Douglas MacBeth and Neil Ferguson, *Partnership Sourcing* (London: Pitman, 1994); Jim Womack and Dan Jones, *Lean Thinking* (New York: Simon & Schuster, 1997).

[4] Books that point to the possibilities of emulating the practices developed in the auto-industry include: Peter Hines (1994), *ibid*; Jim Womack, Dan Jones and D. Roos, *The Machine that Changed the World* (New York, Rawson Associates, 1990); and, Jim Womack and Dan Jones (1997), *Lean Thinking, ibid.*

[5] John Ramsay in "Right to Reply", *Supply Management* (27th November 1977), op.cit., pp.24-28.

[6] A review of the letters pages to the editor in *Supply Management* provides an insight into the practitioner view on the need for a radical reform of the professional role. See in particular the

comments about the IPSERA conference in *Supply Management* (10th April 1997), and the subsequent discussion in the letters pages that followed. The article by Fred Gott, "A Stacked Deck?" *Supply Management* (18th September 1997), pp.40-41 is also instructive about the practitioner viewpoint.

[7] On the problem of benchmarking see: Andrew Cox, *Business Success* (1997), *op.cit.,* pp.1-79; Andrew Cox and Ian Thompson, "Don't Imitate, Innovate", *Supply Management* (30th October 1998), pp.40-42; and, Andrew Cox and Ian Thompson "On the Appropriateness of Benchmarking", *Journal of General Management* (Vol. 23, No. 3, Spring 1998) pp. 1-20.

[8] This is discussed more fully in Andrew Cox, "Clarifying Complexity", *Supply Management* (29th January 1998), *op.cit.*

[9] The research being undertaken on outsourcing at the CBSP is currently published in the following books and articles:

Chris Lonsdale and Andrew Cox, *Outsourcing: A Business Guide to Risk Management Tools and Techniques* (Boston, UK: Earlsgate Press, 1998) www.earlsgatepress.com); Andrew Cox and Chris Lonsdale. "Strategic Outsourcing: Evidence on Business Practice and the Role of Procurement", *(Proceedings of the 6th International Annual IPSERA Conference,* Ischia, Naples, April 1997); and, "Outsourcing: The Risks and Rewards", *Supply Management* (3rd July 1997), pp.32-25.

[10] Originally presented in Andrew Cox, "Clarifying Complexity", *op.cit., p.36.*

[11] On the four principles of effective leverage see: Andrew Cox, *Business Success, op.cit.,* pp.171-190.

[12] See "Right to Reply", *op.cit.,* p.25.

[13] Cox, *Business Success, op.cit.,* pp.133-190.

[14] *Ibid.,* pp.304-306.

[15] "Right to Reply", *op.cit.,* p.29.

[16] A useful warning about the problems of virtual integration is found in: Henry Chesborough and David Teece, "When is Virtual Virtuous: Organising for Innovation", *Harvard Business Review,* (1996) Jan/Feb, pp. 65-73.

[17] Our own research on outsourcing and privatisation provides a useful critique of many of the simplistic views on the benefits of outsourcing. See references in note 9 above and

[18] Andrew Cox, Lisa Harris and David Parker, *Privatisation and Supply Chain Management; On the Effective Alignment of Purchasing and Supply After Privatisation* (London: Routledge, 1999 forthcoming).

CHAPTER 2

THE STRATEGIC APPROACH TO PROCUREMENT AT SMITHKLINE BEECHAM

Mark Ralf

Introduction

In this case study the SmithKline Beecham (SB) experience of adopting a strategic approach to purchasing is discussed. The case study focuses on how to break into new areas of organisational spend. SB is one of the top 12 UK listed companies. It has four main business sectors: Pharmaceuticals, which is the biggest; Consumer Health, which is the over the counter (OTC) medicines purchased at the chemist shop without a doctor's prescription; Animal Health; and, Clinical Laboratories, which is the equivalent of path labs in UK hospitals. In 1993, SB had £6 billion worth of sales and spent £3 billion with external vendors. It is a large company with purchasing teams in 40 countries accommodating approximately 440 purchasing people who do everything from logistics and administration to strategic purchasing.

The original vision of purchasing in SmithKline Beecham was a ladder of progression. This ladder encompassed logistics and administration, automation and delegation, MRP2 systems, right through to purchasing as a business department integrated into a wider business function. Two of the major themes at SB have been "Maximising Profit and Cash Contribution", and the "Widening of the Horizon and Scope of Purchasing" to encompass all bought out spend within the organisation. These two themes are very important because SB has a large non-production expenditure. At the same time, because a great deal of work had already been done in the inventory and production areas to reduce costs and add value, we have recently focused on the non-production spend.

The reason SB decided to do this is related to opportunity and effort. It is possible to work in an area which has reasonable purchasing and, after a couple of man years effort, using high class purchasing techniques, to obtain 5-15% reduction from total acquisition costs. This would be achieved using short-term measures but, as General Motors has already experienced, this has to be paid for in the future. In the long run, however, most finance directors would probably give purchasing an OBE or a knighthood if it could continually take off 5-15% (as well as inflation) in the production areas of spend.

The same amount of effort can, however, be applied to most non-production areas. It is possible for production related systems - MRP2, BPCS, etc. - which normally are only applied to inventory, to be applied to non-production areas of expenditure. There are also many non-production goods and services which are bought in but which purchasing has very little influence over. This trend increases as outsourcing develops. The importance of non-production is therefore growing in line with streamlining activities and world class manufacturing activity. For many companies 60% of the bought out spend with external vendors is in the non-production area. If purchasing does not focus on this it will miss a huge opportunity, and also ignore a fundamental part of the cost base.

The Structures Necessary to Facilitate Change

Purchasing must integrate into the wider business. It should not focus only on those areas where it has traditionally been welcome, because in many cases this is no longer the focus of the enterprise as a whole. General managers and the financial directors of companies accept manufacturing factories and production as a necessary evil, but they are only in those businesses if they can perform better than outsiders. If it is more productive to source outside then the company will do so. It is no longer necessary to own the means of production in order to assure quality.

We use this approach and vision a great deal in SB because, as part of our procurement initiative, we analyse end customer needs and the link from these to SB's own business needs. While every private enterprise has responsibilities to its stakeholders, if companies merely manage their own needs they will lose focus. To obtain the proper focus companies have to look to their own supply base, and also to the secondary supply base which is the supplier's supply base. As companies start to look down this supply and value chain they come to realise that the demand from the customer is incredible: year on year cost improvement, year on year service improvement, year on year quality and innovation transfer. Every time we, as customers, buy a new car we expect more free features and higher standard quality, or we become irritated when things break. We are all part of the problem of customer demand for innovation transfer, and we expect to pay less money for it year on year.

The resulting demands down the supply chain are therefore for quality, innovation and value to the customer. The customer also demands strong cost control all the way along the chain. To achieve this companies have to exploit new opportunities but, in the non-inventory area, one must recognise that the new territory is fraught with danger. Entering into any unknown territory can be dangerous because the indigenous population is often hostile. The average marketing person, for example, will look at the average purchasing person and assume they know nothing about marketing, and therefore cannot help. To an extent this view is correct because if purchasing tries to make marketing decisions it has probably overstepped the mark. But it can be argued that marketing's procurement of goods and services is incomplete if purchasing is not involved. Much relies on the ability of purchasing to become an integral part of teams which otherwise would be devoid of a purchasing input in many areas of spend. There are many 'keep out' signs and there is a great deal of hostility to overcome. Nevertheless it is possible to make progress. In SB we have shown that the problems disappear after a while if the right methods of entry are used.

The standard tools and techniques used in purchasing are not always adequate for this task. It is not possible to apply the standard automotive and inventory type of purchasing practices in non-inventory area. They do not work. Many of these techniques are predicated on a level of control and a continuity of supply which does not exist in non-inventory spend. We have to develop new tools and techniques such as *"opportunity scoping"* to ascertain what budgeting and forecasting savings could be achieved in any area of spend. There are tools and techniques which have been developed in SB which provide indicators as to what these numbers might look like. New thinking and new approaches are required, and this means internal training schemes and the transfer of knowledge rather than a policy of expanding the purchasing function.

In developing our opportunity analysis SB has not used the traditional ABC approach in purchasing because of the level of organisational difficulty that applies when addressing non-inventory and non-production areas of spend. The SB approach has been to say if the opportunity looks good we ought to go for it, especially if it is considered to be strategically important to the business.

In summary, strategic benefit can be added through proficiency and technical competence, but the organisational difficulty is relatively low; these are the areas in which to start. It is essential, however, that purchasing stays out of areas where organisational difficulty is very high until it has gained experience. There is much to be said for delivering small benefits and then coming back to more difficult organisational areas later.

It is important to match skills to the opportunity. SB uses people with marketing or IT skills rather than people with purchasing skills, especially if they have good interpersonal and technical skills. SB feels that it is possible to teach purchasing skills but if someone is lacking in some form of technical skill, or is interpersonally incompetent, it is difficult to teach these to people quickly enough for them to be useful in an era of rapid change.

Strategic Purchasing at SB

Strategic purchasing at SB is organised into two teams - one based in the UK and one based in the US (reporting to corporate level). There is also some strategic purchasing in the businesses, but the remainder of this discussion will focus on the dedicated strategic purchasing teams. The role of these teams is to provide dedicated resources which are focused on non-production activities and they also have time to spend selling the process in the business. Their task is to deliver high value benefits.

The size of our corporate team is predicated on a multiple of fifteen times the units total cost. If an individual costs £40,000, it is expected that this will result in £1 million of total cost being taken out of the business. There are 20 people (10 in the UK and 10 in the US) who introduce innovative purchasing techniques into new areas of spend. The aim here is to create standardised "better practices", rather than "best practice". Most of the strategic purchasing work at SB is related to developing standardised better practices. The goal is reliable purchasing processes and not the creation of purchasing departments everywhere. Overall the aim is to reduce the number of purchasing people in the organisation not to increase them. The only way to do that is by having standardised processes. Whenever SB buys marketing services, or media, or print then it is expected that these standardised processes will be followed.

For new categories of expenditure SB uses a strategic purchasing process which has been developed in collaboration with the corporate purchasing team and an outside consultancy. The aim is to train people once so that marketing people, engineers or technical QAs can purchase professionally themselves with little or no help. This approach has been enormously successful. Once non-purchasing staff understand the process, and have seen it work in a non-threatening area, they are much more comfortable with purchasing something closer to their own business needs.

Built into this strategic process are new tools like *"constituency mapping"*. When dealing with inventory items there is a tendency to fail to consider who influences this process. The focus is often on the people who sign, rather than on the people who have an interest, or on those who are ultimately the end users. Who these players are is well known, well documented and normally written into the specification for inventory items. When dealing in non-production areas of spend there is, however, normally a network of influence which has never been written down. As a result it is possible to plan a cost reduction and value programme only to discover that a key player is able to say no. Unless these relationships and influences are mapped early on there will be automatic failure further down the process. It is necessary to map out the constituency and then tailor the strategic purchasing solution so that it meets the needs of all parties in the process.

Overall our aim at corporate purchasing level is to see that these standardised practices and processes are written up so that they become the current better practice across the four divisions as a whole. Once the system has been endorsed by one division of "non-purchasing professionals", (marketers, engineers and the like) the approach is much more readily accepted in the other divisions. A further caveat must be raised when breaking into new areas of spend and this is the need for an early decision on whether the opportunity is better served by dedicated, sector or by local resource. If someone in one of the businesses is trying to develop a world wide media agency deal, and they are going to devote 10% of their time to it, they will still be trying to do it in the new millennium. More dedicated time is required and, in this example, strategic purchasing would be involved at SB.

It would be a mistake, however, to start strategic purchasing with a worldwide media agency deal because it is just too organisationally complex. The proper way to start is at a country level in order to obtain initial gains and to win the marketing people over. Once everyone can see the benefits of the new approach in the UK and France, they are much more likely to agree to apply it to Spain and Germany as well. It then becomes possible to make a decision about whether it should be set up as a strategic project, because the mechanisms required and the way the market is structured are now known. Having undertaken a *"process design project"* first, (which helps us to understand the nature of this market) a strategic project can then be planned.

Only in this way is it possible to understand the supply chain properly. If one analyses any average product currently being made, particularly in a pharmaceutical industry, it is possible to follow a single supply chain from initial conception right through to end product. This might be done to produce an advertisement for television which involves hundreds of inter-linked supply chains. If a company decided to use a consolidating agency to provide most of these services they would be paying the top rate of commission for all the services provided regardless of the value being applied to them. So in the case of a simple thing like photocopying or couriers, if the average mark up of a media agency is something in the region of 40-50% (and some of them are a lot higher than that), then someone in purchasing might be horrified if someone in the marketing department made an offhand comment about bringing 14 copies to the next meeting, the cost of the photocopies might be 20-30p a sheet. There is clearly a great deal of scope for purchasing to assist marketing to reduce costs in this case. It is essential, however, that this is achieved through consensus at a strategic level.

What a Strategic Approach can Achieve with New Tools

The reason why achieving consensus is crucial is because the goal is to maximise benefits for the business as a whole so as to obtain competitive advantage for SB. The corporate strategic purchasing groups in the UK and US focus on global high opportunity, high value and high service areas, where there is scope for vulnerability reduction, or major cost control. The focus is always on global, cross-sector or trans-regional issues. Many of our projects start, however, in areas where acceptance has been won initially by doing things at a much lower level. In doing this, one must never lose sight of the real goal, which is to be working in strategic rather than peripheral areas. Part of the strategic purchasing process is to map out the portfolios of the strategic purchasing teams, to ensure that they do not gravitate down towards either a low opportunity or sector regional focus. It is very easy for resources to be eaten up in this way, and it is essential to ensure that there are balanced portfolios for these teams.

Using these techniques SB made £24 million additional savings in 1993. This will rise to £35 million in 1994. The strategic purchasing process used is so rigorous that we have a very high level of confidence about these figures. So that, even though it is not possible to say specifically within the individual projects which ones will hit the right numbers, we know that the balanced portfolios will almost inevitably hit the projected savings. This demonstrates the level of confidence we now have with the process.

To make this work, however, it is necessary to develop new tools. In conjunction with the marketing department at SB corporate purchasing has developed a new tool called *"strategic negotiation"*. The aim here is to negotiate with people about the long term relationships. The marketing agency you deal with year in year out may have been decided but how does one obtain a principled negotiation that will last for a long time? With ADR Consultants, SB has developed a package which marketing now uses to train its own staff. Interestingly, the sales force at SB also uses this new negotiation approach as part of their own sales training to understand what is being done to them at the other end of the customer chain.

SB has also developed an approach known as *"negotiation planning and conditioning"* which is used for multi-media. Staff use this approach to practise on before entering into major negotiations. By the end of 1994, through corporate-wide Lotus Notes, we have also developed new tools which will allow every purchasing manager worldwide to see every corporate source plan, contract, supplier, and the names of supplier managers. For SB this will be a revolution through dedication which has been achieved in only 11 months.

Three very different purchasing studies - air travel, duty management and market research - provide clear evidence of the SB approach and what is achievable through dedicated effort in non-production spend. The first case - air travel - is about relationship and control. SB spends a fortune on air travel. Initially SB thought it spent £4 million on air travel but we were wrong by a factor of 10. Being a merged company (a UK and US company) our travel expenditure was spread across 57 travel agencies in the US alone. We did not know where the money was going and people throughout the company had different ways of spending it. Our task in corporate purchasing was to find a partner. We went to a major airline and asked if it could help us to find out what our level of expenditure was, but it refused because it already had most of our business anyway and did not feel the need to deal with us. We were told to come back only when we could move some market share and, thereby, provide more business!

We, therefore, had to find another partner in a relatively unknown global travel agency.   This agency helped SB to control its travel expenditure, and SB now has 99.7% compliance in its travel policy. SB can now shift market share in a way that the airlines understand. Corporate purchasing spent a great deal of time installing the right partner but has had a tremendously beneficial effect on the way SB does business.

SB now has a stable partner but our original strategy was misconceived. Strategic procurement is surely awash with this type of error. We set out thinking that we knew what was needed only to find out that we were wrong.   Our original goal was to obtain an implant from an airline, and thereby, to control our expenditure. From a supplier point of view this example shows that SB is a huge prize which somebody missed because one airline could have owned SB's supply chain. Through ignorance of value and supply chain relationships the airlines turned their backs on millions of pounds of worldwide travel. The cash flow benefits alone from this would have been worthwhile for any individual airline.

The second case study is about duty management. SB spends £20 million a year on duty management, or the paying of taxes for things we have to move around. SB makes a chemical in one place and has to move it for secondary processing and it may have to move it a second time after that. Often, because the sites at which this is done are very specialised, or a supplier sources from Europe into the United States, SB may add value to the product and then sell it on in South America. SB has to pay duty at each stage in the process. The problem is that SB has a wide customer base, and had never tackled this hugely complex problem. SB's problem is that it has to deal with the tax authorities and the regulatory authorities who determine what prices can be charged and, therefore, the tax levels in virtually every country in the world.   SB corporate purchasing put dedicated resources into this problem and, as a result, saved £3/4 million in 1994. It took nearly a year to cut 5% from the total cost but next year it will be possible to save several million because of what was learnt on the way. Corporate purchasing knew that savings were possible but it was not possible to know how much they might be or how long it would take to achieve them.

The third case study is much more traditional and relates to continuous marketing research. This is the type of information that consumer health in SB needs to gain relative market share. SB felt it had a poor service with no synergy and an absence of shared learning. If an employee had information which dealt with exactly the same commodity used elsewhere in the company there was no mechanism to share the learning. In 1994 corporate purchasing dedicated resources to this issue and has already taken 23% out of the total cost. The service is exactly the same, but the application of the service has improved massively. Now that a continuous market research deal is in place, the strategic purchasing team are working to build on developing a principled relationship by which, year on year, the costs will automatically decline.

Conclusions

The closeness of relationship which SB seeks to generate with suppliers over time is not a matter of chance and it is not about development. It is about deciding what the business strategy is, what the strategic sourcing plan should be, and which kind of relationship is necessary. The good old fashioned Rottweiler approach to buying must co-exist, however, with a more collaborative approach internally and externally. This is clearly the point Andrew Cox is making in Chapter 1 when he emphasises the need for a strategy based on competitive and collaborative approaches. Adversarial relationships exist, and rightfully so. What is needed, however, is a balance between both approaches and a sophisticated understanding of which tactic to use to develop the strategic goals of the organisation. Deciding which relationship is necessary and when is crucial. If this is not done then companies can be sucked into relationships they do not want, and that often generates higher costs, or time consuming activities and behaviour that are dysfunctional.

SB has, therefore, found it necessary to educate suppliers to the fact that, in many cases, being a preferred supplier for SB is probably better than being a partner with a company which does not know what the term means. In many cases SB may not want to partner a company in a certain category of expenditure simply because SB does not believe a partnership is relevant for that activity. Whether we have collaborative partnerships or arms length relationships depends on how SB feels any particular relationship will best assist the fulfilment of the strategic corporate goal. This means we have many and varied supply relationships and will continue to do so.

We have found also, as we have moved further into non-traditional purchasing, that there is a tendency for suppliers to design partnerships as a cosy route, or even to look for strategic alliances. In many cases, however, it can be argued that there is no reason why companies would ever need to progress beyond preferred supplier arrangements in many non-production areas of spend because partnerships provide no additional benefits to cost reduction.   At SB, rather than trying to build up a purchasing team or relying purely on partnerships, the bottom line comes down to standardising the processes, dedicating the resources that are applied to them and making sure that these skills are transferred into the rest of the company.

PART B:

LEAN SUPPLY

CHAPTER 3

THE FUTURE FOR PURCHASING: DEVELOPING LEAN SUPPLY

Richard Lamming

This chapter is based upon survey research conducted in the international automotive industry since 1982, and in electronics manufacturers since 1993. In the four years since the publication of 'The Machine That Changed The World' (Womack, *et al* 1990), however, the concepts of lean production have clearly developed to include applications in many other areas, not only in manufacturing. Attention is now focused upon the lean enterprise rather than lean production (see Womack and Jones, 1994). What follows is a discussion about the development of 'lean supply', the supply system that is required to support lean production and the formation of lean enterprises.

The first question that must be addressed is: "Why is there now this increased concern for the strategic nature of procurement: what has changed recently?" Having answered this, we shall consider what lean supply is and how it may be connected to strategic procurement. Lastly, we shall look at what those responsible for procurement must do to achieve lean supply. Many of the aspects of success at Rover Group (see Chapter 4) during the last few years may be traced to development which we identify as parts of lean supply, and it is useful to examine their implementation in this light.

Why is there Concern for Purchasing?

The simplified view of the pressures faced by businesses at the beginning of the 1990s is shown in Figure 3.1.

Figure 3.1:   The Pressures Facing Business Organisations in the 1990s

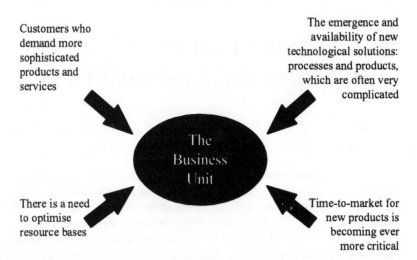

Customers who demand more sophisticated products and services

The emergence and availability of new technological solutions: processes and products, which are often very complicated

There is a need to optimise resource bases

Time-to-market for new products is becoming ever more critical

The four arrows, summarising the pressures, represent business imperatives - unavoidable factors of competition. There can be few, if any, business organisations who have not found their customers becoming more sophisticated, better informed, and harder to please. In selecting the services and goods that they need, customers now have more choice than ever before and are therefore harder to win and to keep. This applies equally to industrial customers, and to that most fickle of animals, the consumer. The arrow in the top left hand corner of Figure 3.1 is thus a pressure that every business recognises. In order to satisfy these new types of customer, firms need clear organisational strategies which will support responses to the market.

The arrow in the top right corner reflects the emergence of readily available technological tools - solutions to problems. These are factors that firms cannot afford to ignore: they are there and they have to be evaluated. Strategists know that if they don't exploit these technologies, competitors probably will. They come in the form of 'hard' technologies such as computers, components or products, and in the form of 'soft' technologies - new ways of doing things. It is vital for firms to know about these technologies - hence the pressure. They may be discarded, or shelved, but they cannot be ignored. Firms must therefore be able to keep their eyes and ears open in a much more broad sense than was previously necessary.

The lower right hand arrow shows the pressure of time. Development processes (i.e. for new products and new operating systems) must be completed in less time than has previously been acceptable, as product life cycles continue to shrink and markets crave cheaper, smaller, lighter, and more powerful products (the personal computer is a prime example of this: it is now necessary to launch new disk drives at half the cost, twice the access speed, half the size and twice the capacity, every nine months).

The last arrow needs little explanation: the need to do more with less-using 'optimised' resources. This translates, for all organisations, into the need for innovative ways of doing things - in some cases fundamentally different from established practice.

The question which this description begs is: "How do organisations deal with this?" The answer is that they cannot. It appears that it is not possible for the traditional company or organisation to manage all of these pressures at once - it was not designed to do that. The shape and structure of today's business organisation has changed little since its origins, one hundred years ago, when customers were not as sophisticated, not so well informed, and accepted that there were limits to what could be provided. They might complain, but they would expect to put up with imperfections. In Rover's case, just having a car seventy years ago would have been a major satisfaction, whereas now, of course, it depends what car it is, how old it is, what features it has, etc.

So the organisations we all currently work for were not designed to handle today's business environment. It is as simple as that. These are the complex pressures which are forcing change in strategic procurement. The inability of organisations to deal with these pressures provides an opportunity for purchasing, because it appears that the way forward requires fundamentally different approaches to inter-firm relationships. The way to face the pressures is to collaborate with other firms and to find new strengths outside the traditional boundaries of the firm. Collaboration is not new, of course, but the urgency and extent of the need to work in this way appear to present managers with challenges which are either new or have not been seen for a long time.

Figure 3.2 illustrates the likely result of this new situation. The business unit is slightly smaller, 'downsized' through shedding non-core activities, but reinforced by strong collaboration with other firms that were once called supplier.[1] Naturally, the business unit needs to collaborate with other firms, perhaps competitors in some cases, leading to some very strange bedfellows. There are many reasons for strategic collaboration, well documented in research, (see Contractor and Lorange, 1988) and most of them apply to the collaborative nature of modern supply relationships (see Lamming, 1993).

Figure 3.2:   Response to the Pressures - Strategic Collaboration

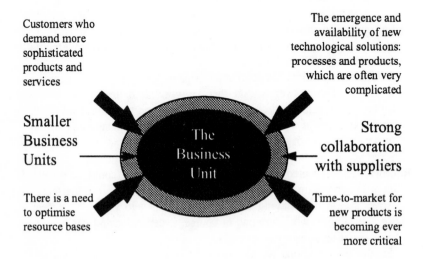

Customers who demand more sophisticated products and services

The emergence and availability of new technological solutions: processes and products, which are often very complicated

Smaller Business Units — The Business Unit

Strong collaboration with suppliers

There is a need to optimise resource bases

Time-to-market for new products is becoming ever more critical

For purchasing, this means an entirely new role in holding together something which has not existed in the past - a complex organisation involving ownership of a centre core and collaborative management of an external organisation. In Figure 3.3, we see the boundary of the traditional organisation, the company, in the inner line, indicating the resources within ownership.   The outer line, bounding the larger shape, is the complex organisation, sometimes called a virtual organisation. This is the extended organisation, which is what the world sees: what competitors, customers, shareholders, politicians and consumers see. It is the extended organisation that all these parties think of as the company, defined by its capabilities. In fact, the company is simply the heart of this organisation: the difference is that around it lie collaborative partners that make it as strong and knowledgeable as it has to be to compete in the business world. This arrangement has been described by various writers - see for example (Handy, 1989, and Prahalad and Hamel, 1990).

Figure 3.3: The Future for Purchasing: External Resource Management

As existing organisational structures prove inadequate, strategic purchasing becomes a matter of managing external resources

There must be complementary assets in the internal and external resource bases. Purchasing and supply becomes:

"External Resource Management"

Source: Lamming, R.C. (1993) *Beyond Partnership: Strategies for Innovation and Lean Supply*, Prentice Hall, page 251.

This means that the business organisations of the future may be expected to have entirely different shapes and forms from the vertically integrated Leviathan model of the mass production company, which most of us, production or service, motor manufacturer or university, represent. The glue which holds these new organisations together will be the strategic relationships between the core and the collaborators - the suppliers of goods, services, technologies, intelligence and competitive strength.

The opportunity for purchasing is, of course, also a threat. There is no guarantee that the people running these vitally important relationships on a day to day basis are going to be those who are currently called Purchasing Managers and Buyers. The traditional Purchasing Officer is not equipped to manage strategic relationships with collaborators. Such responsibilities can hardly be placed upon the shoulders of those who left school at sixteen and have learnt simply by doing, those who gained a qualification after school and assume that will last them the rest of their lives, or those who typically spend less than two days a year in self-development and education. The likelihood is that unless new business skills are developed in these people, they are not going to be able to handle the requirements of the organisation of the future and there will be a steady supply of young MBA graduates with engineering degrees, who would never call themselves purchasing people, ready to move in and run these relationships.

The new strategic function will probably not be called purchasing - that is much too limited a word. The connotations of purse strings and of spending money have no relevance to the setting up and management of strategic inter-firm relationships. This task is concerned with ensuring the correct external resources are in place, to complement the internal resources. Perhaps 'external resource managers' is a term that future purchasing managers may adopt.

This is the future for purchasing. This is why there is this current concern - because its role and nature have to change fundamentally. The names will change, the people may well change. The people with foresight are already changing.

Lean Supply[2]

It is important, at the outset, to bear in mind that the concept of 'lean' management is not Japanese, nor is it about cars, and it isn't solely about manufacturing. The research which uncovered the idea of the lean enterprise began by asking why the Japanese appeared to have a significant advantage in the automobile manufacturing industry (and many others). In order to understand it fully, it is necessary to study the developments in manufacturing paradigms over the twentieth century. These are illustrated in Figure 3.4.

The word 'paradigm' is a much maligned word. It is also a perfectly good word. It means a set of expectations, the factors which one expects to be constants. In manufacturing, this has changed twice during this century. A hundred years ago, products were made in a process which involved skilled people with flexible tools and a lot of collaboration. The expectation was that making something that was complicated, such as a gun, a car or an electrical appliance, required skilled people. Such items, it was assumed, could not be made by unskilled people. This was a paradigm: the expectation that it would need a workshop with skilled people, who had developed through the apprentice-journeyman-master route, the craft Guilds etc., to make complex products. Such a system produced people who were trained for decades to be good enough to make something as technically complicated as a can opener.

At the turn of the century, the North American continent did not have a large number of skilled people. In order to compete internationally, therefore, they had to change the paradigm. They re-invented methods of making things, calling it 'manufacturing', and developed a system which became known as 'mass' production. Changing the paradigm, so that it became possible to have items as complicated as a car made by people who had no industrial skills, was a fundamental innovation. Like all true innovations, it involved destroying the old way - craft based production - in order to make way for a new approach.

Mass production was built upon scientific management which had previously convinced the Americans that workers should simply obey instructions (given to them by managers, who had devised the 'one best way' of completing the task). It was possible, therefore, to use non-skilled people to do what had traditionally been the reserve of skilled people. The paradigm shift was total and it led to the demise of craft production.

The Americans took their new paradigm around the world, bringing about a demonstrator effect: they built mass production plants in Europe and the Europeans copied them. It took Europeans fifty years to develop mass production. By the 1960s, mass production plants were still being developed in Germany, Italy, France and Great Britain. Two entire generations of Europeans had grown up thinking in mass production terms. These include such concepts as economies of scale, accepted as a fact of life, but actually a function of mass production thinking. The practice of giving discounts for bulk purchases is seen as a natural concept, but it is in fact just another example of mass production thinking.

There are many, many more examples. It is almost as if Westerners had come to see people who came to work in factories as unintelligent: they had to be told what to do, and if they objected to established practices, they had to be corrected. This is mass production thinking as well. In developing mass production and thereby destroying craft production, the Americans actually lost a great deal of the value that was in the former paradigm: the product of the intelligence of every individual involved in the process.

Figure 3.4:   The Two Paradigm Shifts in the Twentieth Century

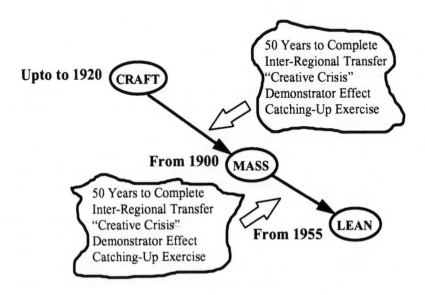

The twentieth century's second paradigm shift in manufacturing began after the Second World War, in Japan. It occurred, just as the first one had, as a result of a set of extraordinary historical circumstances. In the wake of the war, the Japanese had nothing other than their skills, their equity, and their self-respect. With these they developed a new way of running production - a new paradigm which, like mass production before it, was to become pervasive - its influence spreading far beyond the domain of manufacturing. Research has shown that this system uses significantly less of every resource: effort, time, space, and materials, to develop products which provide lean manufacturers with a two-to-one advantage over mass producers: half the effort, half the space, half the development time, and less than half the number of suppliers are required, to produce products with twice the quality.

For the second time in a century, the world saw the spread of a new paradigm. The Japanese found that they couldn't do what they had to do using mass production, so they changed the rules.

Those in the West - in Europe and North America - are now going through the demonstrator effect of lean production, and, indeed, lean enterprise, since the system influences management thinking in a far broader field than manufacturing alone. Manufacturing plants have been set up in the United States, and in Europe, employing lean production - first by the Japanese, and more recently by Western companies who have observed the paradigm shift. Meanwhile, the newly emerging industrial nations in the East, and the re-emerging countries, such as Mexico, Brazil and Australia, are benefiting from the new approach as fresh investment follows lean principles, rather than accepting the outdated ideas of mass production. It is called 'lean' because of the notion of there being no fat in the system, the organisation operates at its 'fighting weight'. It is a system which actually needs less of everything.

Each of these twentieth century paradigm shifts has changed the way companies are configured. There was no company large enough to manage mass production when it was invented and it required innovative thinking on the part of two large finance houses to invent General Motors (Chandler, 1964). It may well be that the mass production shaped company is now dying, to be replaced by different forms. Lean organisations are not massively integrated vertically, they have a great deal of vertical co-ordination but they employ the principles of collaborative networks, rather than the overbearing power of ownership type companies. It is not necessarily a matter of the equity exchanges which the Japanese used to construct such arrangements, although some in the West suggest that this may be so (Burt *et al.* 1993), but there is quite clearly often a 'master-servant' relationship between Japanese firms and their suppliers. It is for these reasons that the co-ordination which is patently essential to lean production cannot apparently be provided by traditional vertical integration.

As noted above, companies appear to be unable to manage their market requirements from the basis of their existing corporate form, manufacturing system and product strategy, and are thus looking for collaboration as a strategic response. Lean production is a system based upon a customer-orientated process logic. It is natural, therefore, that alongside the developments in these business factors there is the need for a development in supply paradigms. Lean supply is therefore the name given to the supply system which is necessary to support lean production (Lamming, 1993).

As Figure 3.5 indicates, inter-firm 'partnership' lies at the heart of craft production, as the system necessary to support the rate of innovation which characterised that period (Abernathy *et al.* 1978). Firms were not large enough to cope with the market requirements and 'technology pushes' on their own and thus had to collaborate. Similar systems are in place today in some industries, and it has already been suggested that this could be the new form of industrial organisation for the future (Piore *et al.* 1984).

Figure 3.5:   Developments in Supply Systems During the Twentieth Century

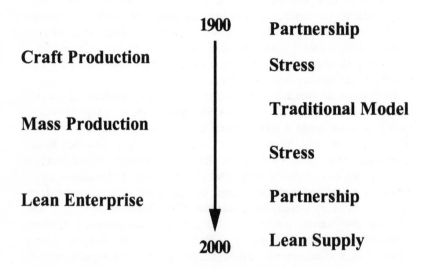

The requirements of mass production did not support this partnership. In developing a system in which customers invested in engineering resources necessary for specifying technical details of parts to be bought in, the mass producers created the purchasing paradigm that would endure for eighty years - that of the supplier expecting simply to respond to the customer's requirements - to the exclusion of innovation on the part of the supplier. Coupled with this technical development was a haughty attitude, clearly evident in the accounts of Henry Ford's activity, which subjugated suppliers to the whim and mood of customers. This was mass production purchasing, it placed stress upon the relationships which had been co-operative until then, and it became what might be termed the 'traditional model' for most of the twentieth century.

The demise of mass production, in the face of markets which were tougher than those for which it was designed, led to stress within supply relationships. Many supplier-customer relationships are still in this stress phase, as the new ways of operating, and new economic models, are forged. Some resolution in this stress becomes evident after a time, as customers realise that suppliers cannot operate without profits, forward planning, and some sharing of risks and benefits. This resolved phase is, however, not strategic, nor deliberate, it is the result of involuntary changes in behaviour (on the part of both buyers and sellers) in the face of economic change. From this state of affairs has arisen the popular concept of 'partnership' within which supplier and customer seek common advantage, from a mutually understood set of shared competitive forces.

In practice, however, partnerships have exhibited quite clear senior and junior partner positions. It may be the customer or the supplier that takes the senior partner role, but in either case, such a situation cannot provide the equilibrium required for a lean logical supply process.

The definition of lean supply, therefore, goes beyond partnership, as it is practically manifested, to a balanced value chain in which complementarity of assets is assured through joint analysis of competencies and investments. The lean supply chain is designed to compete with other supply chains, to win business from the end consumer of the product or service. It is a complex matter, of course, because the suppliers in the chain are involved simultaneously in several other chains - they have to be to become the technical experts which lean supply requires them to be. The jealous guarding of expertise so characteristic of vertical integration cannot be applied in the lean enterprise.

Fundamentals of Lean Supply

The full model for lean supply has already been discussed in depth (Lamming, 1993). In this chapter, we shall examine a few of the key features which have emerged as foci for management attention, since the implementation of the idea began.

Fundamental to the development of lean supply is the identification of duplications. In supply chains, these may take unusual forms which make them difficult to discern. They include such items as invoices, which exist purely to satisfy accountants, expediting (progress chasing), which is a built-in acceptance of inadequacy (and therefore non-competitiveness) and inspection. None of these add value, but all add cost. They are already the targets for removal in many organisations, as part of business process redesign, or re-engineering. The fact that some companies are beginning to work without invoices, expediting, and inspection, means that their competitors can no longer assume that such duplications are inevitable. The need to introduce lean thinking is not optional.

Since supply chains, by definition, cross company boundaries, removal of duplications in them must be a matter for discussion between customers and suppliers. If this discussion is dominated by one side, it will never achieve the aim of long-term sustainable competitiveness for the chain itself (as opposed to success for one company at the expense of others).

Discussion of fundamental business factors which is necessary to bring about such major changes of practice as removal of invoices or expediting is not a feature of mass production supply. Rigorous, enthusiastic, continuous improvement is necessary to underpin such a development - already a problem for firms on an internal basis, and now required between customers and suppliers for the move to lean supply. As many total quality management programmes have indicated, it is possible to change the behaviour of people without altering their basic values - their paradigm. 'Bolting-on' total quality to mass production thinking could never work. Many continuous improvement schemes still do not involve rigorous monitoring of results and therefore lack discipline. For lean supply to be a reality, therefore, it is necessary to install schemes which require customer and supplier to work together with discipline and enthusiasm, without one partner dominating the discussions.

Lastly, lean production and supply challenge a fundamental feature of human mentality, the tendency to make new things fit within existing patterns of recognition. The need to learn constantly is central to lean production, and to learn in concert with suppliers is a fundamental part of lean supply. The traditional approach to new concepts, however, is one of 'smoothing out' factors which contradict conventional wisdom. In this way, people fail to learn from new experience. The practical manifestation of this is the excuse, a common feature of business interactions. Once an excuse can be found for an occurrence (a 'mistake') there is an end to the matter, no potential for learning exists subsequently. The extreme case of the excuse is blame. Once someone can be found to blame for an occurrence, there is a sense of solution (when, in fact, no solution has been found, no lesson learnt). It is common within industry to observe entire operating systems (the 'unofficial' systems) which are designed to rely upon long-standing blame behaviour - sometimes referred to as a 'blame culture'.

Lean production requires the removal of such blame cultures, and for lean supply the same requirement means that companies must install better understanding of each other's perspectives, and internal relationships (e.g. between purchasing and design, or sales and production).

Features of Lean Supply

In order to explain the significant difference between lean supply and its predecessor, some of the key features are discussed below. In almost all cases, these features have yet to emerge in practice, i.e., they are derived from the logic indicated by the research. Implementation of the ideas, however, is currently under examination in several organisations.

The Relationship as a Quasi Firm

The supplier and customer will naturally begin with different perspectives on the relationship, these may represent non-complementary views. Lean supply means that it is the relationship which becomes the entity within which these people, from both organisations, see themselves working. Their job is to ensure that the relationship actually works perfectly and therefore they can see it as some sort of organisation which actually has its own requirements, rights and responsibilities, and interfaces with the customer and the supplier. Their role becomes one of looking at their company from the outside, to ensure that it satisfies its obligations to its partner. The relationship thus becomes a quasi-firm, an organisation within which people work towards its goals.

An example of this developing is given by the case of Bose in the USA, which has suppliers' employees working in its scheduling departments to manage the flow of materials from their suppliers. In this way, the supplier can experience its own service, firsthand. The next step in such a development would be to have the customer's personnel working in the supplier for a while to understand the dynamics there and the implications of policy decision, etc. Finally, the relationship itself would emerge as the entity which must be supported, by whatever resources are required from each company. This arrangement will clearly require funding and should be justifiable on the basis of cost savings and added value which it provides.

Cost Transparency

The concept of 'open book' negotiation is now commonplace in many industries, albeit with many variations upon the central theme. The ideal is that the supplier should explain its process cost structures to the customer, and in return, the customer will help the supplier to achieve cost savings. This notion is based upon the assumption that the customer is capable of helping the supplier, something which is clearly not the case in many industries.

In those sectors where the customer's operation is closely aligned to that of the supplier (such as the automotive industry) it may be assumed that a common understanding of, say, production engineering exists. Furthermore, in such an industry, if the customer firm is larger than the supplier, it may be assumed that the basic tenet of open book applies, the customer should be able to help the supplier. In such cases, too, it will be simpler for the customer to insource attractive business, and thus the supplier is naturally more wary of discussing details of production. This has led to the use of bogus accounts ('two sets of books') and, in some cases, refusal to comply.

Given the need to change the shape of organisations towards lean enterprise, the threat of insourcing must be removed by customers and a move towards genuine sharing of data accomplished. There is, however, the further requirement that given the logic of lean supply chains, the exchange of data must be two-way, in order for both organisations to concentrate jointly on the removal of duplications. Thus, in lean supply, the customer is prepared to divulge data on internal processes (value chain) to the supplier, at the same time as requiring open book dealing. This is indicated in Figure 3.6.

This feature of lean supply represents a profit-sharing initiative, possibly a 50:50 arrangement on improvement activity. Just as the contract between the customer and supplier (which may or may not be a written contract) will contain agreements on new product development, so there must be accord on productivity improvements, and therefore cost reductions, and perhaps annual price drops.

Profit level, traditionally a bone of contention between customer and supplier, may need to be included in these discussions. In the short term, this may mean agreeing a desirable profit level (for the supplier) as a matter of principle. In the longer term, factors such as return on capital employed in the specific business may need to be discussed. Cost transparency may be combined with target costing (starting with the price the market will be prepared to pay and working backwards to the cost for which the item must be produced), once again requiring better collaboration between supplier and customer than has traditionally been the case.

Figure 3.6: Cost Transparency

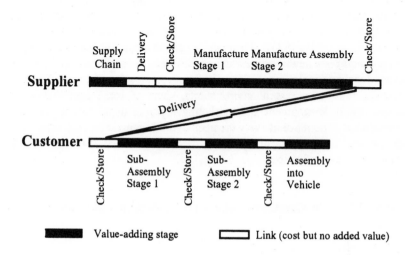

Source: Lamming, R.C. (1993) *Beyond Partnership: Strategies for Innovation and Lean Supply*, Prentice Hall, page 215.

Since customers may buy from suppliers in a variety of industrial and commercial sectors, it may be necessary to consider different cost regimes. For example, a supplier in the electronics industry may need to invest substantially in research and development to retain its position. In this case, a higher profit level may be necessary for the supplier than in sectors, such as metal presswork, which are less technologically consumptive.

The subject of supplier's profit may be expected to provide many difficulties in negotiations, since, as costs are reduced, it is likely that the absolute profit margin will decline and the natural tendency is to protect this. If costs and therefore prices can be reduced, so absolute profits will follow. To reverse this apparently bad performance (in cold financial terms) for the supplier, it may be necessary to increase the overall level of business. This is consistent with the practice of reducing the overall number of suppliers with whom the customer deals (supplier base rationalisation), a process which results in retained suppliers taking increased responsibility for satisfying the customer's needs.

Search and Selection Environments

Lean supply requires exploitation of new technologies. How does a firm ensure that it becomes aware of such matters? The concept of search and selection environments is well established in the literature on innovation (Nelson *et al,* 1977, 1983). The equilibrium which lies at the heart of lean supply requires a new interpretation of this idea, in order to enable firms to expand their technical capabilities. In practice, managers find it difficult to describe their own search environments, short of some combination of research and development and marketing research departments. In fact, the external experience of every member of the organisation may contribute to the search environment, bringing in ideas and opportunities from a broad spread of influences.

Figure 3.7:   The Constitution of a Search/Selection Environment

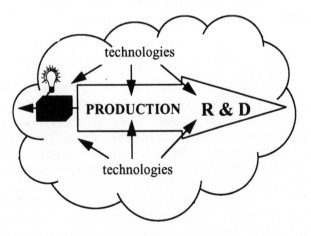

The new collaborative roles within lean supply develop the need for a shared search environment in which the supplier is effectively an intrinsic part of the eyes and ears of the customer. The two companies share the technological knowledge that comes in from the environment. Purchasing must manage this, something which traditionally trained purchasing staff are not generally ready to do. It appears that, as lean supply develops, so companies which fail to build shared search environments will be perceived by suppliers as lacking in interest, and will not realise the potential of technical collaboration.

Relationship Assessment

The essence of lean production and supply is the removal of inappropriate activities. These activities may be wasteful or constraining, or they may perpetuate some non-lean thinking. One of these activities is the practice of vendor (or supplier) assessment, or vendor rating.

The origins of vendor assessment appear to lie in the 1970s automotive industry. In the face of international competition, there was a perceived need to improve product quality, coupled with the recognition that the large majority of parts within the vehicle were manufactured by suppliers, who therefore accounted, collectively, for the major part of the added value in the product. Supplier Quality Assurance schemes, as they were called, were set up to improve product quality, based upon the notion that the customer company was in some way able and entitled to dictate not only terms but also practices to its suppliers.

During the 1980s, this practice developed to include other business functions, first logistics, then technologies, and also business management. As noted above, there was some logic to the argument that a vehicle manufacturer would know the dynamics of component manufacture although the idea wore thin in some sectors, where the product and process technologies differed significantly from those involved in vehicle assembly.

In the first stage in vendor assessment, then, the customer assesses the supplier. In the automotive industry, this system is completely installed, with elaborate procedures with which suppliers must comply[3]. In other industries, particularly where companies have grown rapidly on the wave of a new product technology, many companies are about to embark on the practice, and are designing new vendor assessment schemes that are just like this.

There is a flaw in this level of supplier assessment, similar to that we explored in the discussion on open book transactions, above. Vendor assessment is built upon the notion that the customer can derive benefit from requiring the supplier to improve its operation, without the need for the reverse process to take place. In traditional mass production style, the customer is assumed always to be right, the supplier to be subservient. The customer calls the shots.

During the 1980s, companies began to realise the potential value which might come from inviting the supplier to assess them, in terms of practices which prevented, for example, on-time delivery, quality improvements, and cost reductions. This was usually done, however, in an *ad hoc* manner, in contrast to the sophisticated formality which had built up around the vendor assessment process. This second stage of assessment, however, can be said to have opened the door to two-way collaboration. There was plainly not two-way communication, however, since observed behaviour showed that neither party was genuinely listening to the criticisms of the other.

The logical development from vendor assessment, within the principles of lean supply, is that both partners, customer and supplier, should develop joint approaches to assessing the relationship itself, as a value (and cost) adding part of the chain. This might be called 'relationship assessment' (Lamming, 1993). Such a practice must have assessment devices designed to be used only in conjunction (i.e. customer and supplier together) and will require the levels of communication and joint awareness described above which are the basis for developing lean supply.

Summary: The Future of Organisations and Lean Supply

The research upon which this chapter is based concludes that the paradigm shift which has resulted in lean production and supply represents an imperative, not an option. Organisations may be expected to change in many different ways, but it is clear that the demands upon them will not be met without the collaborative inter-firm relationships which have been described within lean supply, including in many cases the need for operating with status equilibrium at the point of transaction.

The implications for purchasing are clear: the need to build new skills. The skills are those of strategy, technology and, of course, the ability to be 'nimble' and able to change at a moment's notice. If the implications for corporate shape and size are honestly identified as external, i.e. stemming from the opportunities in the supply market, then purchasing has the job of convincing the other functions within the organisation to change also, a task that can only be undertaken in a cross-functional team approach. This will change the internal relationships, a prerequisite for successfully developing the new supply relationships called for by lean supply.

In one recent interview, suppliers complained that they couldn't get to grips with a customer's requirements because it was constantly changing shape; the customer sent the supplier a new organisational chart almost every month. This is the sort of business dynamic which must be accommodated in future. It is market driven and if operating systems (and the expectations which underpin them) are unable to deal with it, they must be changed.

References

Abernathy, W.J. (1978) *The Productivity Dilemma: Roadblock to Innovation in the Automobile Industry*, Baltimore, Johns Hopkins University Press.

Burt, D.N., and Doyle, M.F. (1993) *The American Keiretsu: A Strategic Weapon for Global Competitiveness*, Homewood, IL, Business One Irwin.

Chandler, A.D. (1962) *Strategy and Structure*, Cambridge MA, MIT Press.

Chandler, A.D. (1964) *Giant Enterprises: Ford, General Motors and the Automobile Industry*, New York, Harcourt, Brace and World.

Contractor F.J. and Lorange P. (1988) *Co-operative Strategies in International Business: Joint Ventures and Technology Partnerships Between Firms*, Heath & Co., Lexington MA, Lexington Books.

Handy, C. (1989) *The Age of Unreason*, London, Business Books.

Lamming, R.C. (1993) *Beyond Partnership: Strategies for Innovation and Lean Supply*, Hemel Hempstead, Prentice Hall.

Nelson, R. & Winter, S. (1977) 'In search of a useful theory of innovation', *Research Policy*, Vol 6, No 1, pp. 36-76.

Nelson, R. & Winter, S. (1983) *An Evolutionary Theory of Economic Change*, Harvard University Press.

Piore, M.J. & Sabel, C.F. (1984) *The Second Industrial Divide*, New York, Basic Books.

Prahalad, C.K. & Hamel, G. (1990) 'The Core Competences of the Corporation', *Harvard Business Review*, May-June, 68 (3), pp.79-91.

Womack, J.P., Jones, D.T. and Roos, D. (1990) *The Machine That Changed The World*, London, Maxwell Macmillan.

Womack, J.P. and Jones, D.T. (1994) 'From Lean Production to Lean Enterprise', *Harvard Business Review*, March/April, 72 (2), pp.93-103 .

Notes

[1] Some writers are now suggesting that downsizing may have gone too far in some corporations, leading to so called 'corporate anorexia'. In many cases, however, it is clear that organisations still have a great deal of 'fat' to lose (See Hamel and Prahalad, 1994).

[2] The story of Lean Production is explained in full in 'The Machine That Changed The World' (Womack, Jones, and Roos, 1990), to which the reader is referred for evidence of the summary provided in this chapter. The original work on the development of Lean Supply is recorded in 'Beyond Partnership: Strategies for Innovation and Lean Supply' (Lamming, 1993).

[3] Research (Lamming 1994) in the UK automotive industry reveals that some suppliers have to respond to over twenty different assessment schemes from their customers.

CHAPTER 4

DEVELOPING LEAN SUPPLY IN THE ROVER GROUP[1]

Ian Robertson

Introduction

The concepts of the lean enterprise present a huge challenge to modern industries, a challenge to which few businesses have a readily available and appropriate response. It is important, however, for purchasing professionals to recognise that adapting to these continual challenges is fundamental to the success of our businesses today, and the academic world provides one means by which the key issues may be addressed.

Background to Rover

Rover Group has 34,000 employees worldwide, with many subsidiary companies in distant corners of the world. Annual turnover is £4.3 billion, so it is clear that Rover Group is a major contributor to the UK balance of trade, exporting 41% of 1993 global sales of 450,000 vehicles.

On 31 January 1994, Rover became wholly owned by the German BMW AG group, and it is a source of great satisfaction to the company that the very strong alliance that was formed with the Honda Motor Company has remained intact. This alliance is significant, as several of the activities from which both Rover and Honda have benefited, have been derived from the strength of their relationship, bearing testimony to the success of the real partnerships that exist in modern industry. It is important, however, to recognise that successful relationships can only be achieved with continual nurturing and both parties being prepared to work together to overcome problems that inevitably arise. Just like a marriage, it needs to rise above the everyday stresses and strains and remain true to its ideals in order to realise its full rewards.

The purchasing function plays a particularly important role in the Rover organisation. Annual expenditure is about £3.1 billion, i.e. in terms of overall turnover, 70-75% of the costs of the business are derived externally. This was the primary reason for purchasing becoming a strategic function within Rover Group. It would have been impossible to continue to improve, or to satisfy customers, without having the necessary relationships and processes in place with the suppliers who represent such a significant proportion of costs. 80% of the total is spent in the UK and 90% in the European Union, which is a particular source of pride to the company, (although this was largely through historical circumstances rather than because of any conscious policy). The UK economic climate at the moment, however, presents an ideal opportunity for companies to work more closely with their core suppliers, to their mutual advantage.

For the majority of the 1980s, British Leyland was recognised by most people as belonging to the public sector with expenditure provided by the public purse, at regular intervals and without due consideration to any cohesive long-term strategy or plans. Austin Rover made losses and had very poor industrial relations, the stories of the late 1970s and early 1980s are well documented. The cars were not competitive, and the company image in the market place was very negative. As an organisation, it was based on bureaucracy, fear and inertia. The problems that the company suffered were direct consequences of the top heavy organisational structure with no overriding vision or clear progressive thought. This gradually changed throughout the mid to late 1980s as the company moved into the private sector, initially under the ownership of British Aerospace.

Moving into the mid 1990s, Rover now considers itself to be a completely rejuvenated company - perhaps even a role model for the private sector - being financially viable, producing award-winning vehicles, with desirable brand marques, and nurturing a dynamic and progressive culture. Most important, however, has been the recognition that competition in the industry is ever more aggressive and, as such, one of the key activities for the company has been to survey the market continually for new developments, to ensure that the challenges presented are responded to effectively, for instance through 'Benchmarking' its performance against World Best Practice. It is extremely unlikely that competition will abate in the automobile industry, or industry in general, and it is therefore of the utmost importance to develop successful relationships with trading partners, in order to secure the benefits of strategic collaboration over extended periods.

Total Quality - Strategy & Culture

Back in 1987, Rover commenced a Total Quality Programme, the results of which are now clear for all to see. In recent times perhaps the most significant event has been the 'new deal' for Rover employees which in return for flexibility, provides job security for life. 'Jobs for life', however, does not mean that no-one will ever leave the organisation, but that the people who do choose to leave will do so under their own terms. The concept of job security is derived from the knowledge that if they do their job well, and work at continually improving it, then there will always be a position for them. This may not necessarily be the job that they have always been used to doing, it may involve a change of career direction, but a role will exist. This policy has been of vital importance to the company in terms of alleviating some of the anxiety which arises when making improvements which may ultimately result in people improving themselves out of a job.

Rover Group has now established itself as having some of the most desirable brands in the automotive industry. Land Rover, for example, is well respected in the world of 4 x 4, but it is equally important to recognise the global nature of the potential threats facing the business. It is now becoming a relatively high volume company, moving away from the low volume base which resulted in a considerable stress both for the company and the extended enterprise - its suppliers.

The progressive culture that Rover is now moving towards, which includes such statements of intent as a new deal for the workforce, is part of an overall quality strategy, set out in the late 1980s. The actual name given to quality strategy is not important, and many businesses prefer to use other terms to describe it (e.g. business re-engineering) but, at the most basic level, this involves in-depth analysis of the company and its operations, identifying the key processes and competencies that, if exploited well, will ensure continual company success. These issues may cover a wide spectrum, ranging from quite obvious activities, such as new product introduction, through to corporate learning, the management of people, product improvement and business planning.

Duplication and overlaps have no place in a lean environment. As part of the move to eliminate them, the starting point for a quality strategy is to identify the key driving processes in a business, with clear definition of ownership for each. The strategy embodies an overall vision, which essentially describes how the company or function would appear in a utopian world and, for Rover, each process also has its own 'End Vision', coupled with clear, measurable milestones *en route,* all of which contribute to the identification and elimination of waste within the business.

It is important here to recognise that processes cross previously perceived functional boundaries which have no place in the lean world. The example of invoicing that was given in the previous chapter can be used here. A large proportion of Rover's suppliers are now on direct billing, thereby eliminating invoicing paperwork (though still involving delivery paperwork). A further step currently under consideration is that at the moment a finished car rolls off the assembly lines, each supplying company would receive payment. This is based on the assumption that as the vehicle includes a complete set of components e.g. wheels, seats etc., this is ample proof that the parts have been delivered and received, as such there is no requirement for any surplus paperwork. Naturally, this is only possible if the organisational culture is geared towards it. The elements of mistrust that exist, both internally, and at suppliers, need to be eliminated for this to work, so that people do not feel that they have to ask, "Well, how do I know you haven't lost one?" The culture of the organisation, therefore, has to be that if something goes wrong, then it is 'owned up to'. People must also have the confidence to believe that the company has all the right processes working effectively. Being lean is about taking a step-by-step approach to improving things, and working towards that utopian vision both internally and with your trading partners.

Rover's vision as a company is to be "Internationally Renowned For Extraordinary Customer Satisfaction" - *delighting* the customer. Mere customer satisfaction is no longer enough, most car companies now achieve this. Similarly, since the goal for many companies in the 1980s was to produce quality products as a matter of course, this means that it is more difficult to secure a differential advantage over competitors on the basis of quality alone. As a result, different means to delight customers need to be actively sought. Working towards supplier partnerships, as part of the overall vision and purchasing strategy and objectives, is fundamental to achieving this. Although the term 'partnership' has been often derided, the attitude of companies today must be based on a system of working together with suppliers to achieve a common goal.

The nine key processes that Rover identified for its quality strategy included:

New Product Introduction	Manufacture
Logistics	Maintenance
Sales & Service	Corporate Learning
Management of People	Production Improvement
Business Planning	

A great deal of time was spent by a number of senior executives in the company developing a vision for each of these key processes. This again required objectivity and scrutiny to understand the company's operation fully, in order to decide which processes would make the company a world-class player. The results of this analysis formed the strategy for achieving "World Class Performance".

A further fundamental rule is that if any activity is going on in any area that is not covered within the list of key processes, then it should be dropped. The process either does not add any value, or it is being duplicated, or it is a process that has grown up over history, and an alternative should be found. Given this situation for Rover Group, it was essential that everybody in the organisation from top to bottom understood the terms of reference, and the clear processes that were embodied therein. Equally, some Critical Success Factors were listed, of which one is absolutely fundamental to instigating lean supply: becoming a 'preferred customer'. An organisation can have its own objectives clearly marked out, but unless the right relationships are in place with the right suppliers, (i.e. they consider the organisation to be a preferred *customer*), then the external resources will not be managed optimally - a factor often overlooked, but critical to business success, given the size of the outsourced influence in terms of components supplied.

From the Rover Group Quality Strategy there are clear linkages to the Purchasing Quality Strategy as described in Figure 4.1.

Supplier Rationalisation

Suppliers to Rover have a choice of customers, particularly in the UK, where many automotive companies, such as Nissan, Toyota, and Honda, have been setting up new plants during the 1980s, bringing new revenue streams to the UK. This put the onus on Rover to consider the means by which it might become a preferred customer, and to look at any weaknesses which could detract from achieving this status.

Figure 4.1.   World Class Performance

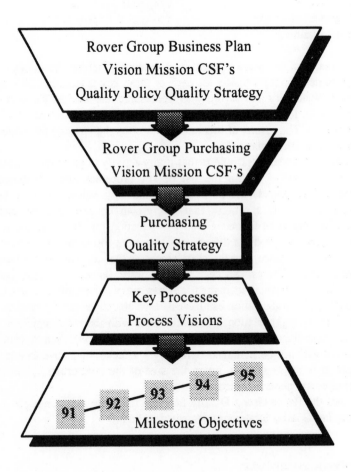

Figure 4.2.   The Purchasing Quality Strategy at Rover

PROCESS	1991	1992	1993	1994	1995	Process Vision							Owner
Supplier Reduction						Fully Optimised Supplier Base	●					●	ISR
Comp. Strategy Dev. & Supplier Selection						Full Alignment to Product and Technology Strategy			●			●	DJH
Supplier Development						World Competitive Supply Base	●		●		●		RB
Total Cost Management						Maximise Material Margins	●	●				●	MMcK
People Development						Multi-skilled, Satisfied and Motivated Staff	●	●			●	●	GBG
Business Planning						Constancy of Purpose	●	●		●		●	ISR
Leadership						Role Models for Continuous Improvement	●	●		●	●		ISR

Purchasing Vision and Mission — Purchasing Quality Strategy — ROVER GROUP (Rover)

One of the fundamentals of this process is listed at the top of figure 4.2: supplier reduction. There is no 'magic number' as to what the ultimate supplier population should be, but with a company like Rover, which has grown from a myriad of companies over a multitude of sites, over many of years, it is not surprising that there were too many suppliers, and little strategic cohesion. Today, this has changed and, whereas at the beginning of the 1980s, there were around 2,000 suppliers by 1990 this had been reduced by 50% and now there are around 700 with a core group of 350 accounting for in excess of 80% of the spend, a proportion which will rise over the coming years.

Of equal importance is the component strategy. Reducing the supply base is only one aspect of the purchasing quality strategy, and although there is no set figure for the level of suppliers to be aimed for, it is imperative to have the forward processes in place, to ensure that not only the right relationships, but also the right technologies support the company's future.

Most importantly, all of Rover's strategic suppliers were taken through the document and the rationale in great detail, so that they all understood the objectives, time frames, and visions for the future. In the same way that the internal teams had been enrolled in it, so the supplier's team had to be enrolled. There are many ways in which that may be done, although the most important elements of openness and honesty must always be present. Accordingly, all relevant parties, both internally and externally, were informed of what was being done, and for what reasons.

The whole process of supply base rationalisation can be very difficult, as inevitably some firms lose out, or will not be considered strategic partners in the future. Every organisation has finite resources, which inevitably results in some competent suppliers being excluded from the Rover supplier list. The policy at Rover has been to be entirely open about this, talking through the reasons, as difficult as they may be. In most cases there was no question of suppliers having done something 'wrong' or having failed to perform, but other companies, at the time, were better equipped to meet Rover's strategic requirements. In removing them from the supplier list, it was acknowledged however that some of these capable suppliers could move successfully into "second-tier" slots in the supply chain, manufacturing parts for direct Rover suppliers. The rationalisation team felt that this was important because Rover had long established working relationships with some of these companies and opportunities might arise in future if, following a suitable development period, the capabilities of first choice suppliers failed to meet expectations.

In terms of the 'ingredients' for lean supply therefore an optimised supply base is of fundamental importance. As mentioned above, there is no finite number: for Rover it is around 350, while for Nissan in the North East it is about 180, in Toyota (Derby) it is around 200. Clearly, this is dependent on a wide range of factors, such as complexity of the product, or the number of vehicle platforms being manufactured.

Supplier Development/Building Relationships

Responsibilities need to be devolved, with supplier companies having the capability to design, manufacture and take overall responsibility for delivering a quality product to cost and time. As at London Underground (see Chapter 7), where trains are currently procured according to cardinal point specifications, Rover's vehicles are procured using a less detailed specification. This means that the Rover engineer can provide details of the amount of space available for a car seat, coupled with some outline specifications referring to whether it should be electric or manual, the type of materials and trim, and then let the supplier design it. This eliminates the need for customer involvement in the design process of intricate parts. In order to achieve this, the organisation must devolve responsibilities which require that the relationship be viewed over a long term perspective. To be successful, suppliers have to become 'enrolled' in the business essentials. Until only very recently, Rover did not reveal its product plans to suppliers until very close to volume production. This secretive approach conferred upon the company extra power over the suppliers, who only found out about the next vehicle or other model to be launched, as the developments progressed. Today, the company enrols many of the strategic suppliers from the initial concepts, relating to plans which have a 10 or 15 year horizon.

Evidently, a degree of trust is required for this to be possible, together with a feeling of shared destiny between the companies, which, in turn, needs to be measured effectively. Single sourcing, for example, is very important to the way in which the company works. Although some commodities such as tyres are multi-sourced, almost all components for Rover products are now single sourced. Placing this level of trust in suppliers can bring significant benefits. The car industry, for example, used to double tool many components, making it easy for supplier A to rely on supplier B if he had a 'problem'. With only one company responsible for the components, suppliers now tend to take a different view, being motivated to find improvements, and thereby helping with cultural change, towards the aspiration of shared destinies.

It is important to recognise that, just as business performance progresses, the relationship needs to be continually nurtured with the same objective. Currently, most supplier development activities in industry tend to be one-way assessments, and at best two one-way communications, in which neither party really listens to the other. Rover is now pursuing a more pro-active approach based on the self-development of suppliers, offering support and coaching where appropriate, while encouraged to review Rover's progress towards its vision of being a preferred customer.

Although much progress has been made towards the vision, Rover still faces problems related to historic sourcing patterns. The supplier base has improved but it is still largely reactive, not proactive, in nature. The company has had to accept that these weaknesses exist but it continually seeks the basic causes (whether they be at Rover or the supplier) and develops plans which will provide lasting improvement and solutions for both parties. Supplier Development programmes, together with enhancements to the Product Development process, continue against a background of long-term planning, continuous improvement, open-book costing, teamwork and common objectives. As such, adversarial relationships with hidden agendas no longer have a role to play in the Rover supply base of today and tomorrow.

It is a particularly challenging task to move towards this goal of fewer, closer, more capable suppliers, the process which is described in figure 4.3. It is, however, difficult to proceed at a uniform pace with all of them, a point to be recognised when these processes are put in place. This goal is, nevertheless, the fundamental building block of everything that Rover is trying to achieve, and the reason it is the top priority within its quality strategy.

Rover's Quality Strategy has played a fundamental role in shaping and delivering the improvements that are visible in the business today. Although it started in 1987, the benefits have only begun to be realised in the last few years, demonstrating that it requires considerable investment and commitment over long periods to make it work. The vast number of hours spent on training alone, for example, constituted a huge investment for the business, yet the results did not become apparent until a considerable way into the programme. The process of improvement continues within a culture of nurturing and leadership, so as to thereby avoid the twin dangers of slipping into decline or being overtaken by competitors.

Figure 4.3. Fewer, Closer, More Capable Suppliers

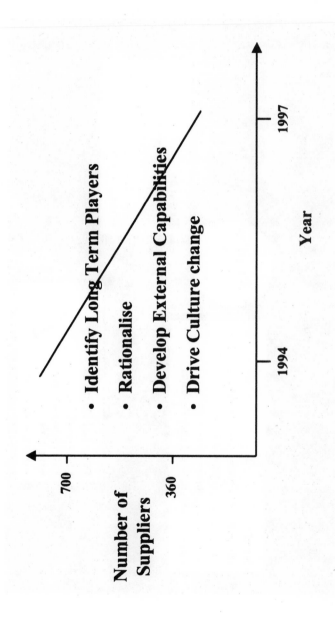

Figure 4.4.   The Road to Culture Change

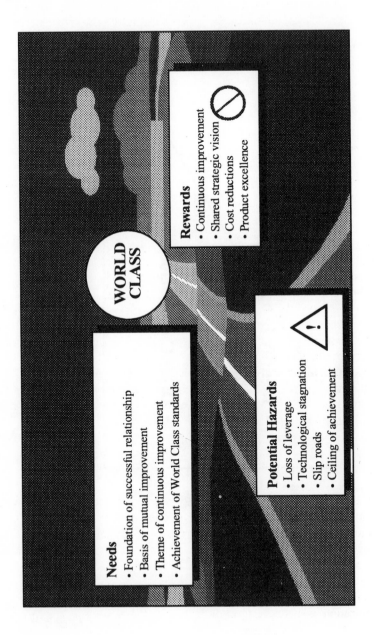

The rewards to both customer and supplier are based on a shared strategic vision, shared cost reductions, and a joint commitment to product excellence. Underpinning all of this is a fundamental commitment to continuous improvement in every aspect of the business. It is now the remit of purchasing professionals to strive for these goals, to measure and recognise their achievements, whilst maintaining a degree of awareness for the potential hazards.

The hazards may be numerous. Loss of leverage can be an issue, not only because customers may feel that they can no longer force suppliers to work on demand, but because not every business will want to work in partnership, perhaps preferring to operate in a more traditional manner. As such, different methods of ensuring that the company moves forward will need to be employed with different suppliers - a portfolio approach. Technological stagnation is also relevant. Some companies may not have the necessary technology or foresight to be competitive in the future. Again, purchasing must nurture the technology progression. For example, if a component design is moving technologically from being metal to plastic, then consultation should be sought with the current metal supplier, as his business is under threat. He may go out of business unless he develops an alternative strategy. The world-class customer must do everything possible to help that supplier adapt to such changes in circumstances.

Close relationships can, of course, lead to a ceiling on achievement: either a partnership reaches its natural conclusion or better ways of doing things become apparent, with both parties going separate ways - an unsatisfactory outcome but one that must be recognised. In summary, the relationship must be continually nurtured to avoid the hazards in order to achieve mutually beneficial rewards.

Internal Relationships

The dynamic nature of today's business environment presents major opportunities for purchasing to redefine traditional approaches to relationships. In terms of the organisation gathering momentum for change it is essential to promote the two-way dialogue mentioned above. Companies must challenge the notion that the customer is always right and can dictate his requirements without discussion and consent. They must, in other words, take on a more interactive collaboration in which the whole organisation is involved. Even the most professional and enlightened purchasing team will not produce the best results without the involvement of other key players, such as product engineers, manufacturing staff and marketeers. If the aim of the organisation is to be responsive to the market place then the purchasing strategy should be meshed with the objectives of other departments and should support the overall goals of customer service. The essence of this Quality Strategy is based on processes not functions or departments. Without this focus, plans inevitably suffer fragmentation, confusion and differences of interpretation.

Resistance to change may well be a fundamental problem within organisations that are trying to instigate lean supply techniques. This manifests itself in many ways and requires senior management to be convinced of the vital role that the purchasing function should play in the future of a successful organisation. Twenty years ago purchasing had limited credibility, due largely to its administrative nature. Today, so much has changed that re-education is necessary throughout the organisation to educate staff and colleagues to the leading role that purchasing professionals are taking in many aspects of the business and the nature of the tools and techniques which are being employed. So many academic and industrial buzz-words surround purchasing today that there is a danger of it becoming isolated and accused of being 'ivory towered'. This may make it difficult to identify short-term direct bottom-line benefit against new concepts and processes. This is in contrast to an engineer, for example, who can give the specific pay-back on an investment in a particular machine. Careful explanation is therefore required to convince senior managers of the need to invest scarce resources in developing the level of strategic awareness and professionalism amongst purchasing staff that is now required to achieve results in today's ever-changing business environment.

In supplier organisations people are generally ready to change. There is a growing recognition of the benefits of partnerships and the frame of mind to discuss new ideas with customers. In the customer's organisation, however, there can be a great deal of scepticism and fear generated because partnership principles demand radical changes to traditional functional rigidities. In steering the business towards process orientation rather than functional orientation it may well be that accountants have to work in one office with engineers, purchasing people or with production people to break up these great silos of functional professionalism, which naturally causes concern to some people. What is required therefore is that the purchasing function actually begins to sell itself to internal customers, initially through well prepared and rehearsed presentations. These presentations need to be built on and proved very quickly, through pilot schemes, where credibility and rapid company-wide successes, however small, can be demonstrated.

Rover conducts Business Reviews with key suppliers in which it involves non-purchasing departments, because it recognises the critical importance of a team approach to building successful partnership relationships. Too often in the past the purchasing department made decisions in isolation from the business as a whole, failing to realise that many of the quality problems, the excuses and the finger pointing were a direct result of this approach. A growing understanding of the need for change was supported by 'customer surveys' to determine people's views of the purchasing department across the organisation. The Purchasing Quality Strategy was fundamental to enrolling the business in a new/developing approach for instance, involving product engineers and manufacturing staff in 'Core Teams' to manage supplier selection and supplier development.

The impact of all this on the personnel profile in purchasing will vary according to the different stages of organisational development. Some companies have greatly increased the number of people in their purchasing departments in order to handle the degree of complexity in managing partnership style relationships with external suppliers. Rover, on the other hand, has been able to achieve significant reductions in purchasing staff. In addition, the purchasing team now includes 'Best Practice' engineers, cost estimators and other skills. Existing and new purchasing staff also receive intensive training to facilitate a broader business approach.

Rover Group Purchasing has a commodity-based structure in which the buyer for tyres has responsibility for all vehicles. This enables a level of knowledge and expertise to be developed so that core teams can be aligned with a single point of contact for particular commodities. To complement this, and running horizontally through the structure, are platform themes, (i.e. specific to the various vehicle families). In these items purchasing 'Team Leaders' work on new programmes within Project Teams, cutting horizontally through the whole organisation. As a result, the company benefits from a matrix approach, while at the same time reaping the benefits of having a single point of contact.

Developing 'agents of change' is fundamental and personnel development is a key process in the Rover quality strategy. Approximately 80% of the purchasing team have now completed, or are in the process of completing, a two year programme of study at Warwick University, covering a wide range of subjects incorporating leading edge tools and techniques to suit today's business needs. This training does not stop there, however, but will continue with other programmes, based at Warwick, Bath and Birmingham. There are also many people on MBAs, MPhil's and various other types of academic training. The idea of agents of change is vital to the way forward, and to the re-focusing of working practices and processes as the company progresses. As Rover moves forward, so relationships change, both internally and externally, and some of the management tools in use may become obsolete. The use of benchmarking techniques have been used extensively to establish new tools more appropriate to our developing needs.

A good example, at Rover, of enrolling the external enterprise in order to encourage a greater feeling of involvement with the product, emerged at a recently run Land Rover workshop for suppliers. Production of the Discovery 4 x 4 model has increased fivefold since launch in 1989 and further significant growth is anticipated over the next few years. This has presented an enormous challenge and some concern to suppliers because components have been facilitated for low volume production and some technologies and tooling may no longer be appropriate. Rover's response has been to share with suppliers the long-range planning assumptions and enrol them in the detailed assessment of a shared business opportunity. The customer and supplier must be able to share issues affecting the future relationship in an open and free environment, thereby determining the best course of action for both parties.

As an extension of this, it is likely that the techniques and processes that a company is currently using may be outdated within a couple of years. It is necessary to adopt a sound process for reviewing this situation. The concepts and tools that have been used to shape the required culture change in Rover are listed in figure 4.5. Supplier networking, for example, has been a particularly useful exercise and, working with Cardiff Business School, the company has set up a network in South Wales. There is also another in place in the North of England. The schemes tend to be geographically based, so that companies in the same region can learn from each other.

Figure 4.5: Tools to Shape Culture Change

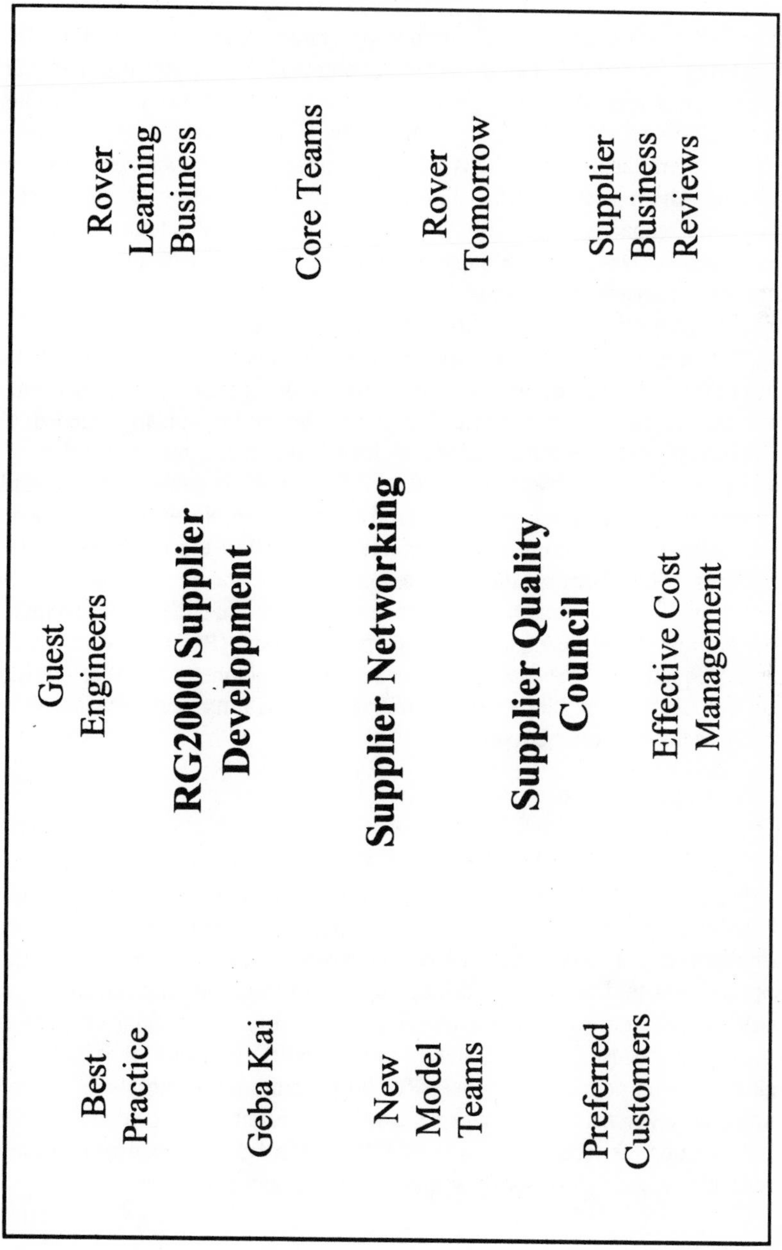

Rover Learning Business

Core Teams

Rover Tomorrow

Supplier Business Reviews

Guest Engineers

RG2000 Supplier Development

Supplier Networking

Supplier Quality Council

Effective Cost Management

Best Practice

Geba Kai

New Model Teams

Preferred Customers

Tools for Change

The 'Rover Tomorrow' programme was fundamental in providing the motivation for radical change across the company. As a starting point for analysis, it involved studying the North American car industry in the 1980s and the advent of the Japanese 'transplants'. The Japanese brought with them a manufacturing capacity of approximately 2 million vehicles per annum, whilst restructuring and plant closures reduced the domestic producers' capacity by broadly the same amount. The salutary lesson in this scenario was that the Japanese brought no new customers. Every Japanese increase in capacity resulted in a domestic reduction because existing domestic customers changed brands and bought Japanese.

The learning from this experience was translated by Rover into a European context and, whilst some obvious differences in the scenarios existed, the basic message was the same: the motor industry needed to understand and embrace Japanese lean manufacturing principles as exemplified by the Toyota Motor Co. There was no doubt that it would happen in Europe because it had already occurred in North America. The motivation was therefore unquestionable, both within the company and at suppliers. The North American lesson, and the vision of what 'Rover Tomorrow' could look like, spawned many of the improvement programmes. The new supplier development model (RG2000) was one of these. Equally, the 'new deal' for workers was fundamental in accelerating cultural changes and introducing increased flexibility and new working practices across Rover Group.

RG2000

British Leyland's 1970s programme of supplier assessment was very much based on compliance. People were sent out on a particular day to check suppliers and if they ticked all of the boxes on their checklist then the supplier was told that they qualified as a quality supplier and left to get on with it. But this was seldom true and the quality of the final product at each stage was usually very different to the quality 'snapshot' that had been taken on a particular day. The ARG100 programme in the 1980s shifted the focus away from compliance towards measurement and became more sophisticated, as techniques such as SPC and Advanced Quality Planning were introduced. However, it was very much a one-way track.

Figure 4.6. Supplier Development

	1970s	1980s	Today
Process	CQC 100	ARG 100	RG 2000
Focus	Compliance	Measurement	Improvement
Requirements	Basic quality systems	Enhanced quality management system SPC AQP	Quality systems Project management Business performance Total quality
Methods	Visit to ensure technical compliance	Technical assessments Warranty performance Delivery performance	BS 5750 Warranty performance Delivery performance Business assessment Improvement coaching

Figure 4.7. Rover Tomorrow: Supplier Led Improvement

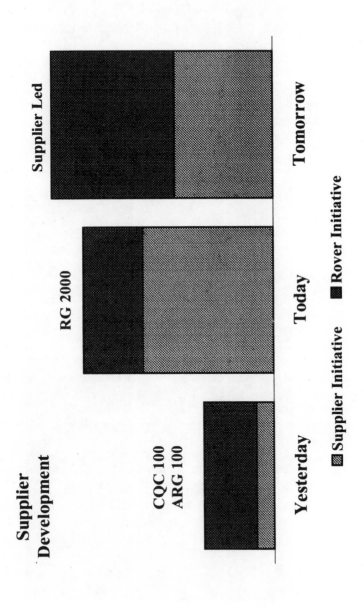

The team of SQA (Supplier Quality Assurance) engineers visited the companies often only to conduct a full assessment, and returned to tackle specific problems with component quality. This process regularly degenerated into finger pointing rather than an analysis of the root causes of failure. Today's priority is about *improvement*. RG2000 is a broad business model, based on self-led improvement. It no longer has the narrow sense of quality measurement which the company used to operate, and it covers every aspect of the business. It is underpinned by total quality measures and represents the first steps required in moving towards some form of 'relationship measurement' for the future.

RG2000 has been instrumental in shaping the required culture change amongst Rover's supplier base. It is a broad business model based on mandatory BS5750/ISO9000 accreditation and incorporates project management, total quality and business performance measures. The standard emphasises strategic issues which are often overlooked, and is designed to encourage both ownership and flexibility in achieving common goals. Its publication is an acknowledgement by Rover Group of the need to form close, lasting partnerships with suppliers to maintain successful, competitive businesses into the next century.

RG2000 assesses and measures suppliers against approximately 350 attributes. Initially, when the programme was launched to sceptical audiences of suppliers the inevitable question to arise from the floor was "Well, what is the passmark then?" The answer to this question is that there is no pre-ordained passmark and it took a great deal of work to convey the idea that they were not being measured simply in order to be awarded a pass or a fail. The point of the exercise was not to punish or reward the company for its score on a particular day but to see how the score could be improved through working together with Rover. The significance of the initiative was that it represented a platform for improvement rather than a snapshot in time. For example, the general attitude is that it is preferable to be with a company that scores 45 and is improving at 20% per annum, than to be with one that scores 50, but is only improving at 2% per annum. Clearly, in the near future, the performance of the company scoring 45 will exceed that of the company scoring 50. This change to the method of assessment, moving away from the pass/fail environment and therefore the stress which was a common characteristic of traditional relationships, has proved an important factor in nurturing a genuine continuous improvement culture amongst Rover suppliers.

There are many measures built into RG2000 but Total Quality underpins the whole assessment. Many companies have embarked on TQI (Total Quality Improvement) programmes and most are aware of their existence. TQI is aimed at turning good companies into quality companies involving all employees (including management) and affects every aspect of a company's operations. In an average company quality costs frequently account for more than 40% of operating costs. One of Rover Group's own quality improvement teams in a paint plant analysed factors causing paint defects on vehicles and, as a result, were able to increase right-first-time quality considerably and to reduce average faults per vehicle by 80%. It is not simply a motivation technique, a productivity programme or a cost reduction exercise, although all of these areas and others will be affected by its continual application. Managers must have strong and lasting commitment to the TQI strategy, providing the basis on which others may build their own convictions and structure their activities. The quality awareness training within Rover Group has considerably increased the expectations of its suppliers, and it is clear that the traditional approach of driving quality performance by increasingly complex quality systems along does not ensure focus on customer satisfaction. The future with Rover Group, therefore, relies on self-motivated, quality orientated suppliers, with whom the company can work in a spirit of co-operation and mutual benefit. The common goals that are established must be designed to increase customer satisfaction continually and to understand, anticipate and exceed customer expectations, while rigorously reducing total cost.

The suppliers to Rover Group today are spread roughly along the full range of the ladder in figure 4.8 (total quality ladder), from traditional through to maturity. It is of equal importance that companies assess themselves in relation to this too, and Rover would consider itself in the learning phase at this time. Seven years down the road from 1987 the company still has a long way to go. There are fewer than a handful of Rover suppliers currently, who have reached the maturity category. These, unsurprisingly, are companies like Motorola who have performed exceedingly well recently and who have been used as a benchmark across the industry. Rover Group set a number of key milestones for moving forward. These have involved winning suppliers over and developing 'hearts and minds' packages, designed to move the few people who were still unaware of total quality away from the traditional category.

Figure 4.8: Total Quality Ladder

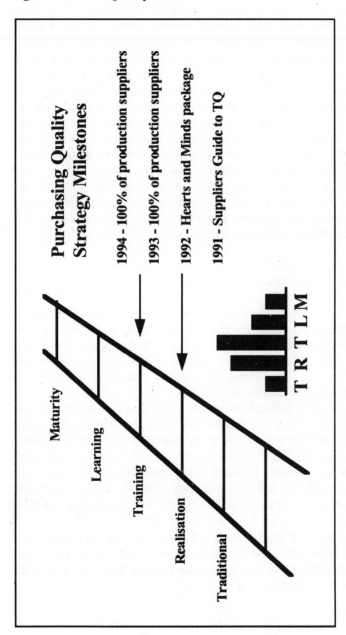

Rover has also offered support and coaching to suppliers in various stages of development. Those companies failing to understand the need for progress have lost out on Rover Group's business. The target now is for the majority of our strategic suppliers to move to the training stage by the end of 1994. The important point here is that the process needs to be continually nurtured. Those companies moving into the maturity category will have a continuing role networking with other companies. The RG2000 programme also has a series of 'Business Effectiveness' measures built in. These measures allow the direct comparison of companies, industry by industry, country by country and location by location. It also provides for an analysis of key strengths and weaknesses by supplier. Using this it is possible to network suppliers who are not in direct competition with a view to improving performance. By achieving and maintaining world-class levels of quality and efficiency suppliers will be in a position to secure long-term agreements with Rover Group and to improve their position with other customers.

The Business Review Process

In order to become a lean enterprise Rover is employing a wide range of tools and techniques. Rover Tomorrow programmes, RG2000 surveys and various networking activities all gradually shift the focus towards joint assessment of the relationship, and through understanding the processes, the 'Best Practice' team should be able to identify opportunities for improvements and the elimination of waste.

To support this, Business Reviews are conducted at regular intervals and involve not only Purchasing but Product and Manufacturing Engineering and others from within the business. The supplier team is normally led by the Managing Director and the review deals with a variety of issues, as seen in figure 4.9, such as the two-way exchange of strategic plans. This process of interchange enables important details to be shared with as wide an audience as possible in order to secure mutual benefit to both parties.

Today, it is commonplace for key suppliers to view clay models of a new car five years before launch, whether or not a programme actually goes forward to production. It was not very long ago when such action would have been seen as complete heresy.

Figure 4.9: Business Review Process

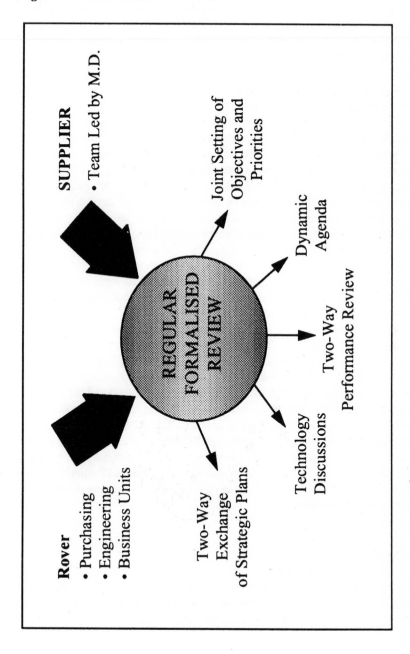

Indeed, many people still believe that it is impossible to share design plans with suppliers because, once that intellectual property is given to a large group of people, someone will breach confidentiality. Properly managed, however, this is an acceptable risk, particularly when viewed in the light of the benefits to be gained by demonstrating involvement and trust in key trading partners. The goals of extraordinary customer satisfaction and lowest achievable cost can only be realised if all of the activities involved in the design, development, manufacture and supply of products are systematically planned and managed from concept through to volume production, with the emphasis on process rather than functionalism.

Business reviews also cover technology. This is crucial because, for example, airbags have moved from a relatively low level of awareness as recently as 12 months ago, to become a part of everyday vocabulary. Most new car buyers either have one or have the option of having one. This choice has, however, necessitated major changes to the body structure of vehicles. This, in turn, has involved continuous advanced technology discussions with suppliers due, primarily, to the ever changing nature of the product as it evolves in size and speed of deployment. An open environment for joint discussion between customer and supplier is therefore vital if companies are to maximise the benefits of evolving technologies and more cost effective solutions.

The discussion forum must be conducive to a *two-way* performance review, 'warts and all'. Rover now has a number of suppliers who have sent their personnel to work in the Rover Purchasing Department. This enables them to become familiar, not only with the company culture and ways of working, but also with the various processes used and the problems experienced with their own company from the receiving end. It is important, however, in this type of scenario, that there is no fixed agenda-it should be dynamic. To reap major benefits from such an exercise it requires an examination of what is appropriate for individual companies at a particular point in time. This individualistic approach equally applies during the important tasks of setting the objectives, choosing the priorities and monitoring progress.

Effective Cost Management

Historically, in the car industry, cost received little attention at the design stage for a new model. This lack of control results in poor control throughout the development process. Consequently, vast amounts of resource were absorbed after the event, (i.e. post volume introduction) to remove costs which with proper and early consideration could have been avoided. This is shown in Figure 4.10, by the step rise in costs at the volume build stage. As a result Rover has developed a culture of cost reduction rather than cost avoidance across the business. The priority has now moved from 'Costing The Design', in favour of 'Designing To Cost'. A simple concept but one which requires very complex processes. The process ensures that suppliers are fully integrated into the Core Team, so that in discussions about new products they understand what the cost of the product has to be in the market place and therefore what the cost targets for their particular component should be.

Figure 4.10. ECM - Effective Cost Management

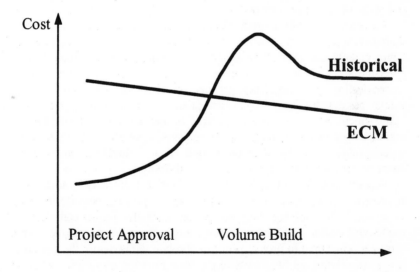

The emphasis is on focusing on best practice at the conceptual stage, rather than trying to regain control of the costs at a later stage, when it is often too late. This involves cost transparency, or 'open book', for key components so as to recognise the finite elements of suppliers cost and in order to find mutually acceptable margins (see Lamming, Chapter 3). Supplier and customer can then work together towards reducing overall costs, to their mutual advantage. This contrasts with the traditional competitive tendering approach which focuses purely on price and results in lower margins not improvements in costs or performance. This very much underlines the principle that the costs should be understood before programme approval and not after the event.

Effective Cost Management is designed to be a win-win activity. With Rover, suppliers are very much involved in this, but it is also important to note that the cost targets are agreed rather than imposed. Component designs are geared towards the optimum cost. Decisions on what can be afforded and a suitable process by which this may be achieved is agreed right from the conceptual stage.

The ECM process eliminates cost throughout the development programme, from design engineering through to materials manufacturing and the full-life costs of supply in the after-market. This is in contrast to previous approaches which often struggled over dividing profit levels at the end of the development process.

There are a number of other ways in which joint improvements may be shared once volume production is underway. With some companies all improvements are split 50:50 basis. This process ensures equality and gives the suppliers more confidence in the customers' commitment to a shared destiny. In terms of new products whole-life contracts often involve annual price reductions. There are other contracts where productivity improvement is built into the contract in the form of rebates against acknowledged or unavoidable cost movements. Overall the focus remains on cost reduction rather than on margin erosion, thereby promoting the openness fundamental to the successful relationship.

Depending on the strength of the relationship there may be those who are reluctant to drive out obvious costs from the process, because in doing so they will be applying their margin on a smaller figure and absolute profits will decline. It may be appropriate in these cases to agree over a short period of time to protect profit in absolute terms, while the customer invests in driving out the excess of the costs from the operation. After an agreed period, of two years, for example, the buyer will go back and review the overall costing structure anyway. This is usually sufficient incentive for the supplier to come to the table and begin to talk about productivity initiatives to drive out costs.

Effective Cost Management is a very intricate and disciplined process and requires the backing of the whole organisation. Underpinning this whole approach is the confidence that new products will be profitable, both for the company and the suppliers, and the recognition that this is essential to their mutual survival.

In terms of selecting future supplier partners and planning joint activities however, Rover Group has had to recognise that ultimately all improvement activities are limited by the suppliers' resources. Many Rover suppliers also supply to other companies such as Toyota and Nissan, who are undertaking similar activities. Careful planning is required, therefore, to ensure that suppliers do not have their resources excessively strained as a result of what other customers are trying to achieve. In addition, it is important to develop a way of working which is individual to those suppliers, enabling them to incorporate all their learning experiences to best effect within their customers' different frameworks and processes.

Conclusion

Defining the company's core competencies and technologies has been the key to understanding where Rover Group is going to be. Ultimately this may involve setting up joint ventures with suppliers. Electronics, for example, is a growth area for Rover and it has been deemed one of the company's core technologies. An area of specialism has therefore been developed for it within the Product Engineering Group. For Engine ECU's (Electronic Control Units) Rover takes prime responsibility for the software engineering and Motorola for manufacture. This enables both partners to utilise a core strength to mutual benefit. With other companies joint ventures involve sharing the risks and rewards. In this instance Rover is developing a new car with a supplier who will be manufacturing the whole body. The body costs a substantial amount of money and there are clearly some risks in this investment.

The closer a company moves towards a mature relationship, the more understanding both customer and supplier ought to have about each other's business and, therefore, a sense of moving towards a shared destiny. It is this feeling, however, that must be understood to be the goal, rather than the joint venture itself, which is actually the means of achieving the goal. Another type of joint venture that is often referred to is that of the Japanese *kieretsu* system. The argument is that unless the customer holds equity in their primary suppliers, it is not possible to achieve such great benefits. Rover does not share that opinion, believing that major customers can reap the benefits without equities or joint ventures; shared destiny is the key.

Maintaining the motivation with suppliers without some form of competitive tension is, however, a very difficult challenge and requires new methods to stimulate progress. Rover has met this challenge with some companies, but not with others. Even the most advanced companies have problems in getting their supply base to move forward at the same pace, e.g. adoption of the Total Quality philosophy. Supplier management capability is also an issue, with TQI being critical to the development of successful partnerships based on continuous improvement. To make progress requires clear, consistent direction and leadership skills which must be continually nurtured. The culture of shared destiny is what all agents of change must focus upon.

Finally, investment in people is of paramount importance. It is the one thing that underpins the key programmes that are being discussed with suppliers. It is a well-worn phrase but British companies have reached the eleventh hour. 'UK Inc.' has a unique opportunity at the moment, with a devalued currency and the growing adoption of some best practices. There is also a flexible and relatively low cost labour force. It is important not to miss these combined opportunities. It is necessary to have agents of change within purchasing groups who will lead the way forward and actually define what needs to be done and provide continuous motivation. Rover has achieved this through its willingness to invest in people, using an established training ladder and its Integrated Management Learning Programme, within which change management skills are nurtured.

Rover has been systematically and pragmatically adopting the principles of lean supply within its supplier base, although it is recognised that it is impossible to have every company progressing at the same pace. Having understood what is involved the future requires progressive tools to support this and new concepts like RG2000 and Effective Cost Management to assist in achieving goals. Investment in people and a constant, gradual evolution of the relationship are the fundamentals on which companies must build. We must be constantly mindful of our vision and fanatical in our pursuit of continuous improvement in everything we do. Only in this way will we be able to ensure that we move forward at the pace necessary to meet the ever-growing demands of today's business environment.

---

[1] This case study was initially edited by Jon Hampson, University of Bath. The editors and author would like to thank him for his help in this respect.

PART C:

PARTNERSHIP AND RELATIONSHIP SOURCING

CHAPTER 5

PARTNERSHIP SOURCING: A MISUSED CONCEPT

Paul Cousins

Introduction

Organisations are constantly looking for ways of becoming more competitive in today's global market place. It is becoming increasingly evident that firms can no longer pass on increased costs to the consumer in the form of price rises, due to highly globalised and competitive markets. Firms must, therefore, become more competitive. This increased competitiveness can be achieved through the adoption of strategic positioning approaches or, if this option is not available, then a cost reduction exercise must normally be followed. The objective of this approach is to enhance the organisation's efficiency by improving the operation of the entire supply chain without compromising quality or service. This strategic approach to purchasing is not new. The idea that purchasing should become a 'strategic' function within organisations was developed by Farmer in the 1970s (Farmer, 1973) and, since then, there has been considerable support for purchasing being seen as a 'value-adding' function to the firm (See Table 5.1 for relevant literature).

In this chapter the concept of strategic purchasing is discussed and then related to the concept of partnership sourcing. The basic argument is that the concept is often misunderstood and, as a consequence, rarely implemented successfully.

Purchasing as a Strategic Function

Table 5.1 illustrates the progression of thinking and empirical research about strategic purchasing. A common theme running through this literature is the view that individual functional goals and tasks should be linked to the overall corporate strategy of the firm.

TABLE 5.1: REVIEW OF STRATEGIC PURCHASING LITERATURE

Author(s)	Methodology	Major Findings
Caddick and Dale (1987)	empirical - case study	Purchasing must develop strategies and link purchasing and corporate strategy.
Spekman (1981)	conceptual	Purchasing needs to be integrated into corporate strategy. First, purchasing must think and develop strategically.
Browning *et al* (1983)	conceptual	Purchasing is linked to corporate strategy because it supports corporate strategy in terms of monitoring and interpreting supply trends, identifying ways to support strategy, and developing supply options.
Burt and Soukup (1985)	conceptual	Purchasing can have an impact on achieving success in new product development if purchasing is involved early in the new product development process.
Landeros and Monczka (1989)	empirical interviews	Purchasing can support the firm's strategic positioning using co-operative buyer-seller relationships.
Carlson (1990)	empirical - case study	Purchasing strategy is important to product development and long-term goals of the firm.
Reid (1990)	conceptual	Purchasing should be involved early in the firm's development of strategy in order to develop strategies that are compatible with the firm's strategic plan.
St.John and Young (1991)	empirical - survey questionnaire	Purchasing, production, and production planning managers agree on long-range strategy. However, their daily activities are inconsistent with the long-range strategic plan.
Saunders (1994)	conceptual	Purchasing is no longer a service function. A discussion of practical approaches for strategic purchasing.
Macbeth and Ferguson (1994)	empirical - case study	Strategic relationship assessment and implementation. Development of internal and external relationships.
Burt and Doyle (1994)	conceptual	Purchasing should become part of the *Keiretsu* approach to the supply chain activities of firms.
Hines (1994)	empirical - case study and interview	Strategic rationalisation of the supply chain - Particularly concerned with the development and application of Japanese supplier association management techniques on UK supply chains.
Nishiguchi (1994)	empirical - case study and interview	Study of Japanese co-ordination of the supply chain for competitive advantage.

Recent research work, based on a survey of 1,500 medium to large sized companies in the service and manufacturing sectors in the UK, found that

42% of respondents had a purchasing strategy (defined as a short- medium- and long-term plan), and of these only 24% had any mechanisms to link it to there overall corporate strategy (Cousins, 1994). This is despite the fact that the literature suggests that the linking of functional and strategic approaches is vitally important. This would suggest that purchasing has some way to go before it is accepted as a strategic function of the organisation.

The second concept often associated with strategic purchasing is 'value-added'. Porter defines this concept in relation to the 'value chain' (Porter, 1985). He points out that it is the combined activities of the firm that allow it to create synergistic[1] returns, thus leading to an increase in competitive advantage. It is these 'synergistic returns' which the concept of value adding seeks to maximise. Purchasing can play a significant role in the facilitation value adding by the creation of cross-functional teams, to improve decision-making capabilities and the flow of commercial information within the organisation (Cousins, 1994a). Purchasing is also a key element in Value Engineering and Value Analysis projects which can also produce major 'value added' benefits for the organisation (Nishiguchi, 1994).

It is evident from current research that the term value-adding means saving money (i.e. reducing cost) for most UK organisations (Cousins, 1994). While this cost reduction is a natural outcome of a cross-functional team approach, it must not seem as the sole aim; rather it is the logical conclusion which arises out of an amalgamation of value-adding concepts. For purchasing to achieve maximum impact within a firm and, thereby, add value, it must have skilled and educated staff. This has not, however, normally been the case in UK organisations but, recently, there have been some encouraging signs (Cousins, 1993).

Figure 5.1 illustrates that there has been a recent increase in the qualifications of personnel entering the purchasing function at buyer level or above. This date has, however, to be correlated with the attrition levels of purchasing personnel and the overall increase in people entering and leaving higher educational establishments.[2] Not withstanding this, it does appear to be the case that the qualification levels of purchasing personnel are increasing. This fact can be further supported by the recent increase in the number of specialised purchasing postgraduate degree programmes. In addition, the retention level of professionally qualified purchasing personnel (i.e. CIPS professional stage and above) would appear to be very high. It is important to note that most respondents interviewed for this research felt that purchasing offered them a solid career path. They also

felt, however, that they often had to move to different organisations in
order to make any career progression.

**FIGURE 5.1:   CHANGES IN BUYER EDUCATIONAL LEVELS
                 1980-1993**

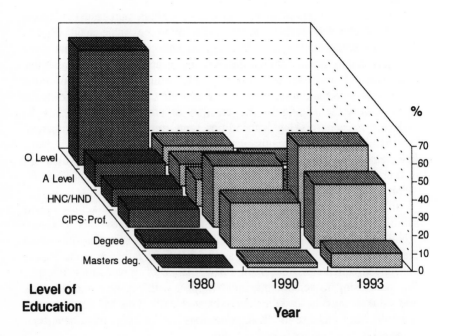

Source, Cousins, P., 1993

Given this increase in the quantity and quality of purchasing personnel
the capacity for the function to become involved in strategic level
purchasing is improved. This means that more sophisticated purchasing
strategies - like partnership sourcing - can be devised. Before they can we
need first to understand what the concept means.

The Problem of Defining "Partnership Sourcing"

Many people believe that partnership relationships occur solely between buyer and seller organisations (Cousins, 1994). This is, however, only one element in the equation (see figure 5.2). In addition, customer/seller interface in the value and supply chain also needs to be linked (B1). We need to address the issue of what it is that the customer actually requires? The most important aspect of relationship building is, of course, the need to integrate internal organisational functions; without the internal integration and co-ordination of functions it is impossible to create a coherent and efficient relationship strategy. Weakly co-ordinated internal relationships lead to miscommunication, a failure of understanding and an inability to match organisational goals to functional strategy and, as a consequence, an overall inefficient use of organisational resources.

FIGURE 5.2: VALUE CHAIN ANALYSIS: INTEGRATION OF THE PARTNERSHIP SYSTEM

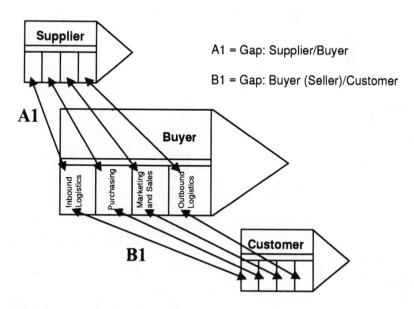

A1 = Gap: Supplier/Buyer

B1 = Gap: Buyer (Seller)/Customer

Source: Developed from Porter, 1985

Firms, when considering their sourcing decisions tend to concentrate on three main attributes: price, delivery, and quality and usually in that order (Cousins, 1994). For complex sourcing relationships, such as "partnership sourcing", many more attributes need to be considered. A total of ten attributes may be of importance in such relationships; these range from objective (easily measurable) to subjective (difficult to quantify criteria). Table 5.2 illustrates the defined attributes[3], which are the basis of a Vendor Management Model (VMM) (Cousins, 1992).

TABLE 5.2: THE VENDOR MANAGEMENT MODEL - USER WEIGHTS DEFINITION

Attribute (A_i)	Attribute Name	Attribute Description
1	Price	The overall cost of the part or project being purchased.
2	Delivery	The lead time for delivery and terms of delivery.
3	Quality	The level of quality expected from the supplier - usually referred to in terms of defect rates.
4	Innovation	How innovative is the supplier? Do they come up with new and original ideas on a regular basis?
5	Level of Technology	How technologically complete is the supplier/buyer? Do they have systems that can sufficiently integrate? Are they a market leader, follower etc.? Do they have a key technology that could be utilised by both parties i.e. Competence in composite technology?
6	Culture	What are they like? Can they be trusted? Is it possible to work closely with these people?
7	Commercial Awareness	How good are they at contracting? Are the contractual arrangements going to be stringent or are they looking to move towards more simplified arrangements?
8	Production Flexibility	What is the current and foreseeable capacity loading of the supplier/buyer? Will they be able to cope with increased order quantities, changes in delivery scheduling?
9	Ease of Communication	Do they have sufficient integration of communication systems both inter and intra organisationally to allow for the free flow of information? Do they operate a 'gatekeeper' system for partnering?
10	Current Reputation	What is their current reputation in the market place? Are they financially stable?

The key points of the VMM are that:-

- It is a standardised system that offers equity in terms of supplier selection to all suppliers. Usually, after the process, all suppliers are given feedback with regard to their performance, outlining why they have or have not been chosen.

- The process does not stop at the selection of suppliers but it continues to manage the relationship over time. It is this feature which differentiates the VMM from other vendor selection mechanisms.

- The VMM changes over time with attributes being added and deleted from the process.

- The VMM is extended both backward and forward throughout the 'value chain' system.

The major barrier to the understanding and implementation of partnership sourcing relationships arises from the fact that the term "Partnership Sourcing" has become perhaps one of the most misused and abused concepts of the 1990s. The word "Partnership" can be found in many company accounts and marketing and sales literature, and even governments and educational establishments now use the terminology in the hope of gaining competitive advantage at a national level. The problem is, however, that the concept has become so generalised that it risks becoming a meaningless concept. One definition is given below:

> "Partnership sourcing is a commitment by customers/suppliers, regardless of size, to a long-term relationship based on trust and on clear, mutually agreed objectives to strive for world-class capability and competitiveness".
>
> (Sir Derek Hornby, Director General, Partnership Sourcing).

There are however numerous definitions of the concept and this has led organisations to assume that "partnership sourcing" means nothing more than having one supplier in a cosy relationship. Such definitions give the practising manager little assistance in implementing partnership strategies because there is a gap between the theoretical approach level and the practical application of the theory to real business problems. The result is that the managers conclude that this simple thing called 'partnership' is very complex and that it requires a myriad of purchasing approaches for each supplier.

In reality it need not be complex. The selection of suppliers for "partnership sourcing" strategies does not have to come from the high cost side of the supply base. Partnership suppliers are simply thos who offer to add the most value to an organisation. The term "value" is very important here because it can refer to a variety of cost elements. Value can be derived from improvements in inventory control and quality and delivery performance, as well as from synergy's created from innovation and joint risk sharing agreements. In summary, one may conclude that it can be applied to those relationships in which there are major "value adding" benefits when all the ten attributes discussed in the VMM above are considered. As we can see in the Case Studies in chapters six and seven partnership relationships can be achieved quite easily and with major benefits for value and costs.

A second problem in successfully developing partnerships is the view that this is normally only a relationship between a Buyer and Supplier. It is clear, however, that to be successful the relationship must also be developed throughout the supply and value chain. It is equally important to understand customer's requirements and to pass these through to the supplier (making the firm proactive as opposed to reactive) as it is to concentrate on the supply relationship above. Equally it is crucially important that relationships are cemented internally so that the internal functions of the organisation are pulling in the same direction. This is probably the most crucial factor for success: without this internal relationship in place there is a tendency for a failure to share information to occur and for communications to breakdown. This results in suppliers receiving conflicting signals which undermine relationships.

Conclusion: How to Make Partnerships Work

It follows from this that if "partnership sourcing" strategies are to become central in the future then the importance of the Purchasing function within organisations must increase. Proponents of this view argue that it should become a 'strategic' function, because it can add value to the organisation, through the findings of cost savings, by co-ordinating project teams, by assisting with innovation and by managing inventory requirements. The current economic climate has, however, forced strategic purchasing to be seen predominantly as a cost reduction vehicle. Despite this many "leading edge" firms have begun to make Board level appointments for Purchasing Professionals as they recognise its long-term strategic importance to the organisation.

As the Case Studies in chapters six and seven reveal Purchasing Managers can make the most of newly found status within organisations to add value and reduce risk. They are beginning to adopt and develop new strategies which focus not only on adversarial cost reductions but on the development of joint innovation, the sharing of design capabilities, and the sharing of quality and delivery performance standards to create inventory reductions with their suppliers. These relationships are by their very nature partnerships because they are long-term rather than short-term. How the development of these types of relationships will affect the scope for manoeuvre by firms in the future is, of course, another question. What seems clear at the moment is that partnerships are yet another tool available to managers in their search for competitive advantage.

Bibliography

Ackoff, R. (1971) 'Towards A System of Systems Concept', *Management Science,* 17 (11), pp. 661-671.

Adamson, J. (1980) 'Corporate Long Range Planning Must Include Procurement', *Journal of Purchasing and Materials Management*, 16 (1), pp. 25-32.

Anshen, M. and Guth, W.D. (1973) *'Strategies for Research in Policy formulation',* Journal of Business, pp. 449-511.

Ansoff, I. (1965) *Corporate Strategy*, London, McGraw-Hill.

Aoki, M. (1988) *Information, Incentives, and Bargaining in the Japanese Economy,* Cambridge University Press, UK.

Arnold, U. (1989) 'Global Sourcing - An Indispensable Element in World-wide Competition', *Management International Review*, 29(4), pp. 14-28.

Birts, A. & Cousins, P.D. (1994) 'Purchasing Partnership, Technology & Treasury Function', *Journal of Logistics*, Summer.

Blau, P.M. (1964) *Exchange and Power in Social Life*, Wiley, New York.

Brans, P. and Vin Due, J. (1985) 'A Preference Ranking Organisation Method', *Management Science*, (31) June, pp. 647-656.

Browning, J.M., Zabriskie, N.B. and Huellmantel, A.B. (1983) 'Strategic Purchasing Planning', *Journal of Purchasing Materials Management*, Spring, pp. 19-24.

Burt, D. (1984) *Proactive procurement: The key to increased profits, productivity and quality*, Englewood London, Prentice-Hall.

Burt, D. and Doyle, M. (1994) *The American Keiretsu: A Strategic Weapon for Global Competitiveness*, Illinois, Business One Irwin.

Burt, D. and Soukup, W.R. (1985) 'Purchasing's Role in New Product Development', *Harvard Business Review*, September-October, pp. 90-96.

Caddick, J.R. and Dale, B.G. (1987) 'The Determination of Purchasing Objectives and Strategies: Some Key Influences', *International Journal of Physical Distribution and Materials Management*, (17) 3, pp. 5-16.

Cali, J. (1993) *TQM For Purchasing Management*, USA, McGraw-Hill.

Carlisle, J.A. & Parker, R.C. (1989) *Beyond negotiation: customer-supplier relationships*, John Wiley & Sons Ltd, UK.

Carlson, P. (1990) 'The Long and the Short of Strategic Planning', *Journal of Business Strategy*, May-June, pp.15-19.

Carlzon, J. (1987) *Moments of Truth*, New York, London, Harper and Row.

Cavinato, J.L (1991) 'Integrating Purchasing into Corporate Strategy', *NAPM Conference Proceedings*, pp. 130-34.

Chandler, A. (1977) *The Visible Hand: The Managerial Revolution In America's Business*, Cambridge, Mass, Harvard University Press.

Chao, C.N. and Scheuing, E. (1992) 'An examination of the relationships between levels of purchasing responsibilities & roles of those in purchasing decision making', *1st PSERG Conference*, Glasgow.

Clark, K.B. and Fujimoto, T. (1988) Lead Time in Automobile Product Development: Explaining the Japanese Advantage, Working Paper 89.033, *Harvard Business School.*

Clarke, K. (1989) 'Project scope & project performance: The effect of parts strategy & supplier involvement on product development', *Journal of Management Science*, Vol. 35, No. 10, October.

Contractor, F. and Lorange, P. (1988) *Co-operative Strategies in International Business: Joint Ventures and Technology Partnerships between Firms*, Lexington, Mass, Lexington Books.

Cook, R.L. (1992) 'Expert systems in purchasing: application & development', *International Journal of Purchasing and Materials Management,* Fall.

Cousins, P.D. (1991) 'Choosing the right partner', *Purchasing and Supply Management,* November.

Cousins, P.D. (1992a) *'Multiple Criteria Decision Making: A practical approach'*, University of Bath, Working Paper, May.

Cousins, P.D. (1992b) 'Purchasing, The professional approach', Purchasing and Supply Management, September.

Cousins, P.D. (1992c) 'Purchasing, the missing link in the information system chain', International Operations: Crossing Borders. North-Holland, UK.

Cousins, P.D. and Dooley, K. (1994) 'A multiple criteria approach to partnership sourcing strategy', Conference Paper, Acrubia, Portugal.

Crosby, P. (1979) *Quality is Free: The Art of Making Quality Certain,* New York, London, McGraw-Hill.

Cusumano, M.A. (1988) 'Manufacturing Innovation: lessons from the Japanese auto industry', *Sloan Management Review,* Fall.

Cyert, R. and March, J. (1963) *A Behavioural Theory of the Firm,* Englewood-Cliff, N.J., Prentice-Hall.

Davis, O. (1985) 'Strategic Purchasing', in Farmer, D. (1985) *Purchasing Management Handbook,* London, Gower Publishing Co., Ltd, Chapter 3.

Davis, T. (1993) 'Effective Supply Chain Management', *Sloan Management Review,* Summer, pp. 35-46.

Dean, J.P. and Whyte, W.G. (1958) 'How Do You Know If the Informant Is Telling the Truth', *Human Organisation,* (17).

Deming, W. E. (1986) *Out of the crisis: Quality, Productivity and Competitive Position,* Cambridge, Cambridge University Press.

Derose, L.J. (1991) 'Meet To-day's Buying Influence with Value Selling', *Industrial Marketing Management,* May, 20(2), pp.87-90.

Dobler, D and Burt, D. (1990) *Purchasing and Materials Management,* 5th edition, New York, London, McGraw-Hill.

Dore, R. (1973) British Factory-Japanese Factory. Berkeley, University of California Press.

Dore, R. (1983) 'Goodwill and the Spirit of Capitalism', *British Journal of Sociology,* (34), pp. 459-482.

Elliot-Shirecore, T and Steele, P. (1985) 'Role of Purchasing in Company Survival', *Purchasing and Supply Management,* December, pp.23-26.

Ellram, L.M. (1990) 'The supplier selection decision in strategic partnerships', *Journal of Purchasing and Materials Management,* Vol 26, No 1, Winter.

Ellram, L.M. (1991) 'Key Success Factors and Barriers in International Purchasing Partnerships', *Management Decision*, 29(7), pp. 38-44.

Ellram, L.M. and Carr, A. (1994) 'Strategic Purchasing: A History and Review of the Literature', *International Journal of Purchasing and Materials Management*, Spring, pp. 10-18.

Farmer, D. (1972) 'The Impact of Supply Markets on Corporate Planning', *Long Range Planning*, 5(1), pp.10-15.

Farmer, D. and Taylor, B. (1975) *Corporate Planning and Procurement*, London, Heinemann.

Farmer, D. (1981a) 'Input Management', *Journal of General Management*, 6(4), pp.3-15.

Farmer, D. (1981b) 'Seeking Strategic Involvement', *Journal of Purchasing and Materials Management*, 17(3), pp. 20-24.

Farmer, D. (1981c) *Insights in Procurement and Materials Management*, West Yorkshire, MCB Publication.

Farmer, D. and Taylor, B. (1975) *Corporate Planning and Procurement*, London, Heinemann.

Farmer, D. and A.R. Ploos Van. (1991) *Effective Pipeline Management*, Gower Publishing Co. Ltd, UK.

Ford, I.D and Farmer, D. (1986) 'Make or Buy - A Key Strategic Issue', *Long Range Planning*, 19(5), pp. 54-62

Ford, I.D. (1978) 'Stability Factors in Industrial Marketing Channels' in *Industrial Marketing Management*, (7), pp. 410-422.

Ford, I.D. (1980) 'The Development of Buyer-Seller Relationships in Industrial Markets' *European Journal of Marketing*, 14(5-6), pp. 339-353.

Ford, I.D. (ed.) (1990) *Understanding Business Markets*, Academic Press, London, UK.

Ford, I.D., Lamming, R.C., and Thomas, R. (1992) 'Relationship Strategy, Development and Purchasing Practice', *IMP Conference*, Lyon, August.

Ford, I.D, and Saren, M.J. (1994) *Networks, Technology and New Product Development.*

Fried, C. (1982) *Contract as Promise*, Harvard University Press, Cambridge, Mass. M.A.

Hamel, G, Doz, Y and Prahalad, C. (1989) 'Collaborate with your competitors and win', *Harvard Business Review*, January-Febuary, pp. 133-159.

Hamel, G. and Prahalad, C. (1993) 'Strategy as Stretch and Leverage', *Harvard Business Review*, March-April, pp. 75-84.

Helper, S. and Leone, R. (1990) 'Strategic Procurement: Using an administrative function for strategic advantage', *University of Boston, School of Management*, Working Paper 90-57.

Hewitt, D. (1989) 'Developing self-supporting Suppliers', *Purchasing and Supply Management*, August, pp. 34-36.

Hines, P. (1992) 'Studies in the East', *Logistics*, February pp. 22-25.

Hines, P. (1994) *Creating World Class Suppliers: Unlocking Mutual Competitive Advantage*, Pitman Publishing, UK.

Hill, R. (1972) 'A Changing Role for Purchasing', *Management Decision*, 10, Winter, pp. 269-282.

Ikeda, M. (1990) 'A Japanese Model for the Evolution of Sub-Contractors', *The Journal of Economics*, 31(5-6), pp. 91-104.

Jones, C. & Clark, F. (1990) 'Effectiveness Framework for Supply Chain Management', *Computer Integrated Manufacturing Systems*, (3) 4, pp. 196-206.

Jones, C, Gore, M, Salt, D. and Saunders, M. (1987) 'Vendor Rating', *Purchasing and Supply Management*, November.

Kanter, R.M. (1983) *The Change Masters*, London, Unwin Hyman Ltd, UK.

Kanter, R.M. (1989) *When Giants Learn To Dance*, London, Simon and Schuster Ltd, UK.

Karlin, S. (1959) *Mathematical Methods and Theory in Games, Programming and Economics*, Addison-Wesley, Reading, Massachusettes.

Kiser, G.E. (1976) 'Elements of Purchasing Strategy', *Journal of Purchasing and Materials Management*, Fall, (12), pp. 3-7.

Kolay, M.K. (1993) 'Supplier Asset Base - Appreciating or Depreciating', *International Journal of Operations Management*, (13) 8, pp. 72-86.

Kono, T. (1984) *Strategy and Structure of Japanese Enterprises.* MacMillan Press Ltd, Hong Kong.

Kraljic, P. (1983) 'Purchasing Must Become Supply Management', *Harvard Business Review*, 61(5), pp.109-117.

Lamming, R.C. (1993) Beyond Partnership - *Strategies for Innovation and Lean Supply*, London, Prentice Hall.

Laneros, R. and Monckza, R.M. (1989) 'Co-operative Buyer-Supplier Relationships and a Firm's Competitive Strategy', *Journal of Purchasing and Materials Management*, (25) 3, pp. 9-18.

Macbeth, D. and Ferguson, N. (1994) *Partnership Sourcing: An Integrated Supply Chain Approach*, Pitman Publishing, UK.

Mintzberg, H. (1983) *Power In and Around Organisations.* Englewood-Cliffs. N.J., Prentice Hall.

Monczka, R.M (1992) 'Integrating Purchasing and Corporate Strategy', *NAPM Conference Proceedings*, pp. 1-6.

Nishiguchi, T. (1994) Strategic Industrial Sourcing: *The Japanese Advantage*, Oxford, Oxford University Press.

Porter, M. (1980) *Competitive Strategy*, New York, The Free Press.

Porter, M. (1985) *Competitive Advantage*, New York, The Free Press.

Sako, M. (1990) *Prices, Quality and Trust: Inter-firm relations in Britain & Japan*, Cambridge, Cambridge University Press.

Saunders, M. (1994) *Strategic Purchasing & Supply Chain Management*, London, Pitman Publishing.

Shapiro, R.D. (1986) 'Towards Effective Supplier Management: International Comparisons', *Harvard Business School* working paper. (9-785-062)

Shapiro, B. (1987) 'Close Encounters of the Fourth Kind', *Harvard Business School*, Working Paper.

Syson, R. (1992) *Improving Purchase Performance*, London, Pitman Publishing.

Williamson, O.E. (1975) *Markets and Hierarchies*, New York, Free Press.

Womack, J.P., Jones, D.T. and Roos, D. (1990) *The Machine That Changed The World*, New York, Rawson Associates.

---

[1] The term synergy, refers to the 'sum of the parts being greater than the whole', or as Ansoff puts it 2+2=5 (Ansoff, 1964).

[2] The level of people entering higher education as a percentage of the total population in 1980 was 5%, in 1990 it was 28% and 1993 it is expected to be around 30% (this includes Polytechnics, Universities and colleges of higher education). Source: CSO statistics.

[3] This research has produced a methodology and computerised tool which enables firms to implement, measure and manage partnership sourcing relationships.

CHAPTER 6

VENDOR ACCREDITATION AT ICL: COMPETITIVE VERSUS COLLABORATIVE PROCUREMENT STRATEGIES

David Mannion

Introduction

ICL is a leading information technology company specialising in systems integration in selected markets. Operating in over 80 countries with 24,000 employees, it generated revenues of £2.6 billion in 1993. Through its services and product businesses ICL also provides its customers with long-term support and access to the widest range of technology. ICL's purchasing spend is £1.3 billion per annum of which fifty percent is spent in non-production or non-traditional spend. The only constant in ICL is change. As the company constantly changes in line with business market-place requirements then purchasing has to change with it.

This chapter addresses the role of strategic purchasing and the influences of best practice on the procurement function. It highlights the importance of providing a value-adding service. Clearly when we talk about Lean Enterprise we must also ask the question whether procurement has a role of its own? Everyone has to buy, but why does it have to be the procurement organisation? If it cannot be demonstrated that procurement adds value then we are not providing a service and someone else will be doing it for us in the long-term! In this chapter the subject of supplier management and the role of procurement in helping differentiate between competitive tendering and collaboration through partnership approaches are discussed, in the context of ICL's overall strategy of elevating the purchasing function to a more professional and core business role.

The ICL Approach to Elevating Purchasing's Role Within the Organisation

The way ICL has managed to elevate the role of purchasing strategically within the organisation is similar to the approach taken by London Underground which is discussed later in chapter 7 and highlights the point that Andrew Cox has made about external shocks, i.e. the crisis suddenly creates the opportunity. In 1981, ICL was a mainframe computer manufacturer supplying a proprietary operating system to a captive market, the British Government. The concept of open tender had been phased out in both national and local government and the company suffered badly, leading to near bankruptcy. The government rescued ICL but at the same time they made it quite clear that the market place would continue to be open to competitive bids and competitive tenders. A new Chief Executive and a new Chairman were appointed and shortly afterwards they appointed a new Purchasing Director. One of his first tasks was to pull together the strategic suppliers (purely manufacturing suppliers at that time) to tell them that ICL had not gone out of business, they would get paid, and that it was crucial that they should continue to supply products.

ICL were reliant upon strategic suppliers because without the technology we could not move forward. We had a dependency relationship. In this supplier conference ICL explained its new mission, requirements and, first and foremost, the importance of the supplier and continuity of supply. This was the start of the recognition of the importance of purchasing at senior management levels. Prior to that point purchasing had been a de-centralised, clerical function. The new Purchasing Director brought a centralised purchasing organisation quickly to bear.

At the same time, the company adopted a philosophy of graduate recruitment. This policy continues to the present day and graduates moved into purchasing from day one. There has been a high retention rate of graduates in purchasing and this has made a significant contribution to developing the function. ICL is a company committed to *Investing in People* and to giving their staff the opportunities necessary for training and development.

By the middle of the 1980s, however, ICL realised that an increasing amount of its spend was being incurred with non-manufacturing suppliers. The total spend for major line items was tracked from the company's invoice approvals database and there was a focus on, for example, utilities, company cars, catering etc. This research provided opportunities for purchasing to become involved in the process and to make a significant initial contribution to reducing costs and adding value. The company has continued to focus on total spend and this has been critical because non-production spend has increased in percentage terms year on year. It is not easy to install standard purchasing practices in non-traditional purchasing areas however, but to overcome this problem an internal purchasing code of practice was developed. It drew upon best practice experiences developed along with a simple flow diagram which explained the basic philosophies. Purchasing experts were then transferred into various parts of the business to help implementation. This process has been very successful but in some parts of the company there is still a great deal of work to be done to implement best practice.

In search of best practice ICL has focused on purchasing as a strategic function. Some of the well-known three letter acronyms have made a major contribution in this development. The basic total quality management (TQM) principle of defining requirements, and of measuring and reviewing performance, are essential to purchasing. Business process re-engineering (BPR) is nothing more than questioning whether any role or function adds value. If you are not adding value then you must be adding cost, and therefore your function is not really required. Investing In People (IIP) is essential if purchasing is to attract and retain a high calibre staff. EQA (European Quality Award) self-assessment is less well known but is arguably even more critical to the success of purchasing. Having experienced the problem that ISO9000 does not guarantee a quality product or service, ICL has chosen self-assessment as the process to focus the purchasing function on.

Self-assessment is a business management technique used as part of a continuous improvement process. ICL has been using self-assessment since 1991 as part of an improvement process focusing on business and organisational development which began in the early nineteen eighties. Self-assessment is not a new concept. In any organisation, analysis of the current situation against planned goals is fundamental. There are many self-assessment models but the best known are those of Deming, Baldrige and the European Foundation for Quality Management (EFQM). ICL has adopted the EFQM model. It imposes a framework for critically examining the company's methods and performance.

Figure 6.1.   The EFQM Self-Assessment Model

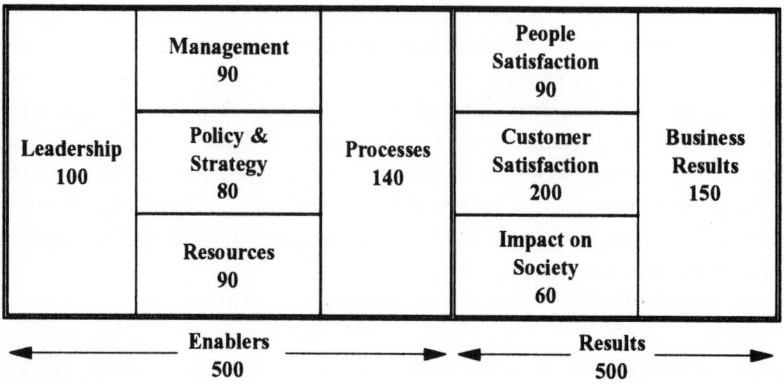

Leadership 100	Management 90	Processes 140	People Satisfaction 90	Business Results 150
	Policy & Strategy 80		Customer Satisfaction 200	
	Resources 90		Impact on Society 60	

◄──────── **Enablers** ────────► ◄──────── **Results** ────────►
                500   500

Purchasers should now be encouraging all strategic suppliers to adopt self-assessment. We should not make the mistake of assuming that this is only achievable in manufacturing processes. All service providers should be encouraged to implement the process in the same way that we, as purchasers, have influenced our suppliers to adopt quality systems and processes. The advantage of self-assessment models is that they look at the enablers of change and the results of company performance. The enablers of change address quality culture and processes but, of equal importance, are result-orientated aspects such as financial performance and customer satisfaction. Under self-assessment the latter is considered to be the most important element and, as a consequence, many companies have implemented just this aspect as an initial step towards improvement. The total approach must be useful however if the model is to work effectively.

The reason for moving towards self-assessment is that it is far easier to ask the supplier to demonstrate how they continuously measure how they meet their customer's requirements than customer generated performance measurements. The approach allows companies to benchmark their performance against the model and therefore demonstrate how successful they are at meeting their customer requirements. Gone are the days of supplier assessment when the customer sent out teams of people to undertake supplier quality audits. We now need to be dealing with companies which are leaders in their own industry and whose leadership is based on self assessment. This is particularly true when looking at strategic and/or collaborative suppliers.

Benchmarking is the term often used for companies striving to achieve 'best in class' performance. Self-Assessment is the ultimate benchmark, but what contribution to strategic purchasing do competitive and process benchmarking make. Benchmarking a company's performance against best in class can be a powerful tool for those still struggling to elevate purchasing to a strategic level. A word of warning however, benchmarking can be quite costly and in fact many consultants are generating a great deal of business through offering to do it for you. ICL has used process benchmarking to deliver the major benefits. Numbers and statistics are fine but we believe that you need to understand the process detail behind them if you are to act strategically.

Process benchmarking works through meetings with peers from other organisations, be they competitors or not, and comparing processes and performance achievement. Building up a network of contacts through organisations such as CIPS in order to find out, for example, who is perceived to be implementing EDI effectively, or who is performing strategic supplier management the best, is one way forward in this respect. Only by talking to others is it possible to assess your own company's performance in comparison. In some cases it might be pleasantly surprising to see how well your company is performing; if not you will learn new techniques and/or come to understand how much continuous improvement is really needed.

The Lean Enterprise as described by Richard Lamming in chapter 3 is an extension of Business Process Re-engineering (BPR) and this brings with it the risk that, ultimately, procurement as a function may disappear. This in itself should drive us to deliver added value as Andrew Cox indicated in chapter 1 in his discussion on value chain positioning.

ICL have recognised this need and have decided that their strategic role is to become a niche player in the IT market, delivering solutions which service the Personal Computer market. A key market requirement in this sector is immediate, off the shelf delivery. This was a major challenge not just in the UK, but it was a fundamental challenge for ICL in overseas markets such as the Asia Pacific rim. The initial strategy was to devise a handling-customer-order fulfilment, warehousing and despatch approach. After value chain analysis we decided this was not the way forward and an opportunity to outsource that part of the business, using a freight supplier who had a track record in handling, warehousing and despatch, was found. ICL decided to work with an accredited supplier who was prepared to develop the customer order processing element to complement their existing services to us. Another example from the UK was the decision to buy one of our value added re-selling customers and then let them handle the distribution of all our Personal Computer products in the UK.

ICL's approach to adding value overall is to try to position purchasing so that it provides a service to internal budget holders. Purchasing has to demonstrate that it is offering the best possible deal otherwise budget holders will question what added value is being provided.

ICL's strategy is to consider the clerical aspects as non value adding and therefore to simplify and/or to automate them. Simplification comes from business re-engineering, while automation is provided through Electronic Data Interchange (EDI). ICL has radically automated its purchasing and supply processes in recent years. The systems in use include the creation of a Master Production Schedule (MPS), the adoption of Materials Requirement Planning (MRP), the elimination of purchasing requisition, the placement of orders and amendments using EDI and, finally, the introduction of electronic Kanban. The latter is an expert system which eliminates unnecessary MRP driven changes and provides the supplier with immediate awareness of ICL's MRP requirements. This enables the automatic authorising of new deliveries and provides total visibility of current and future planned stock against order requirements. (An EDI-Kanban system at Avery-Berkel is discussed in some detail later in chapter 11).

ICL's Approach to Competitive or Collaborative Supply Relationships

ICL's approach has not been to favour either type of supplier relationship. Whether it is a competitive or collaborative relationship the underlying supply and sourcing principles are the same. There is a need for a common supplier selection process initially and this may well be based on competitive processes, but it is the level of detail that is dedicated to the attention to detail with the collaborative supplier which is crucial. All suppliers need to be assessed. Competitive suppliers need to be assessed against three measures: a key quality measure, a measure of unit price and a service measure. An arms length competitive relationship may be chosen because the company cannot afford the management time and attention given the relative importance of the product or service supplied to the total business process. Collaborative relationships are chosen when the goods or services are of key importance to the total business process. When collaboration takes place ICL normally considers the total cost of ownership so as to be able to focus on targeting significant improvement in terms of bottom line contributions to purchasing. Total cost of ownership means breaking down quality, cost and service into detailed sub-criteria, setting objective performance criteria and holding regular reviews of supplier performance. This is a true process of continuous improvement.

At ICL the tender process is similar for both competitive and collaborative relationships. Many organisations believe that the tender process is in conflict with the development of close long-term relationships with suppliers. This stems from the belief that close long-term relationships mean single sourcing, long term contractual commitments and no, or infrequent, market testing. The reality is that successful companies have already grasped the need to seek total cost of ownership benefits by working more closely with many of their suppliers. In some cases, this may lead to single sourcing or the signing of long-term contracts, which is justified on the basis of the produce or service being procured. The norm, however, is for relationships to be developed with dual and or multiple sourced suppliers. The phrase long-term is more often a statement of intent with contracts limited in their duration and still subject to market testing. Close long-term relationships can develop, therefore, even with market testing and competitive tendering.

ICL commits itself to the development of close long-term relationships with Accredited Suppliers, provided they continue to meet exacting requirements in quality, cost and service (Total Cost of Ownership). The contractual commitments entered into are designed specifically for the specific products or services. Suppliers are fully aware that ICL expects them to be competitive and the tender process is often the means for establishing this competitiveness. Service providers enjoying a long-term contract also have to recognise that market testing will continue periodically, throughout the life of their contract. Accredited Suppliers should have nothing to fear from a properly constructed tender because ICL's commitment to them in the long term is based on their continued competitiveness. If they are proven to be uncompetitive then they will be disqualified however long the relationship may have been in the past.

ICL has also tried to segment its purchasing using Pareto analysis. Pareto analysis (80 percent of the value derived from less than 20 percent of the volume) means that developing collaborative relationships with strategic suppliers ensures that purchasing management time and attention is focused on the lion's share of all purchasing spend. ICL's strategic partnership programme is the *Vendor Accreditation Framework*. It was launched in 1991 and currently has 190 suppliers participating and accounts for 75 percent of ICL's total procurement spend. Collaborative partnerships are not restricted to just the manufacturing arena. ICL has 45 of those 190 partnerships with service providers.

ICL has a history of supplier conferences and this has been the vehicle by which it has launched, promoted and given recognition both to the partnership relationships and those partners who have gone the extra mile towards meeting ICL's objective performance requirements. Partnership certificates are awarded, making a public declaration of the relationship and of the period the relationship has been in existence. Awards are made and presented to 'the best of the best' on an annual basis. These supplier partnerships are not just rhetoric. Confidence, trust and long term relationship are all developed through tangible benefits to both ICL and the supplier. The ICL Vendor Accreditation Framework is a management process for the selection of strategic suppliers. It provides an evaluation and performance review process delivering quantifiable benefits for both ICL and each individual supplier. Vendor Accreditation enables ICL to focus management attention on the development of business relationships with a smaller number of suppliers which implies a concentration of spend as the supplier base reduces.

MEMBERSHIP SELECTION

- **Commitment to Quality**
- **The Environment**
- **Industry Leader**
- **Information Systems**
- **Commitment to Europe**
- **Financial Status**

Suppliers are initially selected against six objective membership criteria. These criteria assess the suppliers' business competence and compatibility with ICL and ensure that any relationship is sustainable. When selecting suppliers for strategic partnership, ICL firmly believes in a selection process of the company first and foremost. This process is in advance of, and totally independent from, any specific product or service evaluation. In a collaborative relationship, ICL would look to influence a supplier to emulate the standards that they have achieved against the above criteria. The emphasis is on influence (i.e. these are the benefits ICL have achieved). There is also recognition that ICL may itself learn from a collaborator.

Each individual product or service is evaluated against ICL's objective requirements for quality, cost and service equating to Total Cost of Ownership. Since ICL has the objective of increasing the value of spend with fewer suppliers, measurement is favourably weighted towards multi-range suppliers. Ultimately it is the company that is accredited but it is the individual products or services that are approved, disqualified and/or requalified.

Objective performance measurement criteria are developed by involving each of the discrete business functions (e.g. development, production, purchasing etc.) and these are consolidated within an umbrella points based scheme where quality, cost and service are measured. Measurement is specifically customised to the category of product or service being evaluated. Service level agreements are negotiated with the supplier and fully documented. All performance measures have to be with the agreement of the supplier and not unilaterally imposed. Part of the negotiation task is to persuade the supplier to commit to competitive performance targets.

It is the line responsibility of each function, or business division, to define the requirements, set the measurement criteria, agree the weightings and to subsequently measure performance. This promotes ownership and integration of Vendor Accreditation into the mainstream business processes.

Regular performance reviews are held with the suppliers to monitor performance so as to determine corrective actions where necessary and agree joint actions to improve the business processes for both companies. These meetings are chaired by an ICL supplier manager, who is the owner of the supplier relationship, and who co-ordinates attendance by the relevant line managers involved from the other ICL business functions. This promotes a culture of continuous improvement.

Figure 6.2.   Customised Measurement: The ICL Framework

Customised Measurement

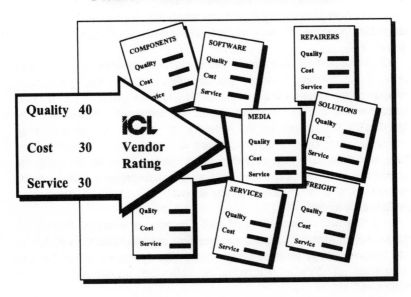

The benefits to the supplier are based on the provision of dedicated ICL management focus. An open relationship is established based on sustained information sharing. Suppliers recognise the benefits of working within ICL's rigorous approach as it improves their own company performance and delivers benefits to all of their other customers and gives them a competitive advantage which helps them to grow their business.

BENEFITS FOR VENDORS

- **Appointment of Vendor Manager**
- **Greater visibility of ICL's forward planning**
- **Joint quality improvement teams established**
- **Provide the right ICL management audiences for Vendors**
- **Increased internal and external awareness**
- **More business**

BENEFITS TO ICL

- **Focused ICL attention and efforts towards key vendors**
- **Vendor confidence and trust in ICL**
- **Vendor awareness of and measurement against ICL's key performance**
- **Vendor actively involved in ICL's quality improvement process**

ICL benefits by having a structured approach to the management of fewer but better Accredited Vendors. This enables concentrated attention to the process of continuous improvement and delivers ICL and its customers significant improvements in quality, cost and service.

Conclusions

This case study demonstrates that ICL, through its Vendor Accreditation Framework and its refocussing on purchasing as a core business activity after 1981, has not only achieved significant gains for the business by adding value and reducing costs but it has also started the process of recognising the strategic contribution which purchasing can make to company performance.

CHAPTER 7

MANAGING SUPPLY CHAINS: A COLLABORATIVE PROJECT BETWEEN LONDON UNDERGROUND AND THE SUPPLY CHAIN MANAGEMENT GROUP

Christopher Bouverie-Brine and Douglas K. Macbeth

The case study is presented in three sections. The first sets the background framework for the project, particularly the evolution of supply chain thinking in London Underground Ltd (LUL). Section two discusses the nature of the process being followed and section three discusses the results and looks to the future.

Section 1 Background to London Underground Limited and the Project

London Underground Limited is a major public sector organisation with a legal obligation to provide a metro service to London. This statutory duty follows the establishment (in 1984) of London Regional Transport, which is the parent organization of LUL.

Table 7.1 shows the dimensions of the company. It is the effective provision and utilisation of our asset base that enables LUL to deliver our 'product' which is a transport service. As a public sector organisation LUL has had an historic tendency to do everything in-house, beginning from development and prototype build of assets; and only going to the market for the mass production of those assets.

TABLE 7.1: Dimensions (1993)

726	million customers per annum
3.5	billion customer miles per annum
245	miles of track
10	operating lines
248	stations
3900	railcars
367	lifts and escalators
19000	staff
turnover	£ 1 billion
g.t.f. assets	£10 billion

FIGURE 7.1: SUPPLY CHAIN PRE 1988

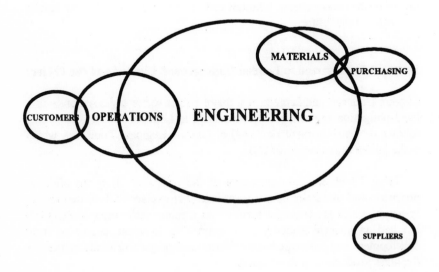

Figure 7.1 shows a schematic of the supply chain and the relative interfaces and strengths of participants prior to the tragic and traumatic King's Cross fire on 19th November, 1987, which resulted in the deaths of 30 people. Prior to that event engineering had been central to the whole process and the other functions were fragmented and certainly not focused on customer (i.e. traveller) satisfaction. It was primarily a railway engineering system that incidentally carried passengers.

Part of the aftermath of that tragedy was the realization of the effects of not focusing on customers and the service delivery operation. This resulted in a paradigm shift in the company's purpose: to be a provider of public transport by utilising a railway system. A further consequence was Government funding of £250 million to support expenditure on new technologies in the form of safety related capital equipment over the following five years.

Figure 7.2 shows the changed supply chain relationships post King's Cross. Suppliers, while now recognised as more important because they bring new technology with them, were still largely held at a distance in traditional adversarial, rigid contractual relationships.

FIGURE 7.2: SUPPLY CHAIN POST KINGS CROSS

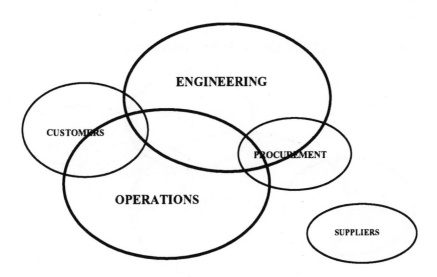

Other influences emphasised the need for LUL to develop new supply chain relationships. One was the nature of the annualised grant funding from Government. Because this funding was often delayed until well into the existing financial year, there was a tendency to buy quickly on price in the few remaining months. It was difficult in such an environment to consider whole life costing. A further influence was the finding (in 1990) by the Mergers and Monopolies Commission of under-investment in London Underground over a 30 year period, causing capital investment to be found from within the maintenance budget to the detriment of existing assets. The MMC also criticised the lack of managerial control and the lack of a commercial ethos, allied to over-centralised decision making.

In 1991, a new company plan was devised which devolved the assets to the operation divisions and was followed by changes in work practices and staff reductions. These changes created a much leaner company. Devolution of purchasing was part of that process. Decentralisation was not seen as a problem as analysis had shown that 80% of commodity spend matched with particular customer groups. Within three months, 50 buyers and support staff moved to 30 business units, with only 3 buyers remaining at the centre responsible for the small value, rapid response business. The remaining staff at the centre have responsibility for procurement strategic planning and the development and the setting of professional standards and the monitoring of compliance with them. (See figure 7.3 for the new supply chain.)

FIGURE 7.3: SUPPLY CHAIN POST COMPANY PLAN

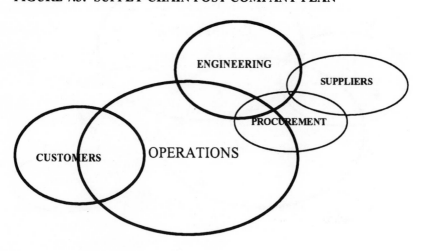

The devolution of procurement was not without its problems. While internal customer satisfaction was high, there were now 30 messages coming from LUL to common suppliers. The centre had to create common systems for the business units. The monitoring of competence within 30 devolved teams of 1-16 people, and the standards to which they were operating, were other issues to be managed. Effective measurement systems were needed. Compliance with EC procurement regulations was of high and continuing importance, along with which came the need for a consolidated supply base across all of the dispersed groups.

With these changes LUL realised the opportunity to improve relationships with its supply base; but with 30 groups, each having critical suppliers, this created a list of 1100 key supply organisations. This number was difficult to manage, because it effectively meant 30 different supplier management initiatives in LUL!

In surveying the external market for an experienced consultancy to address the issue of supplies management, British Rail's involvement with Arthur D Little was recognised as a valid comparator. Subsequent work with ADL created what is known in LUL as the '7-box model' of supplier management, shown in figure 7.4. In a number of the 'boxes' LUL felt that they performed well, in others not so well. A need to focus dedicated staff on specific sectors of the external supply market was also identified.

FIGURE 7.4: 7-BOX SUPPLIER MANAGEMENT

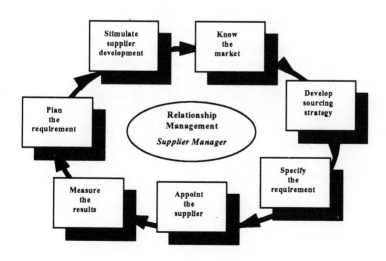

Having established a supplier management vision, the problem became one of how to implement it. At the time the supplier management concept was being developed, LUL had also refined a vision of a Decently Modern Metro (DMM) (See Table 7.2).

TABLE 7.2: A Decently Modern Metro means:

- **New and refurbished trains on all lines**
- **More frequent services, faster journeys and less crowding**
- **High quality stations providing greater capacity and better standard of service**
- **reliable lifts and escalators**
- **new travel opportunities**
- **Rebuilt track and restored embankments, tunnels, drainage, etc.**
- **Better information for customers**
- **A safe, secure environment for customers and employees**

The DMM vision implied Government support for a major capital investment programme over a ten year horizon. The government initially supported the investment level, but subsequently reduced its funding commitment. This prompted the need for much higher levels of cost saving, and a drive to deliver the DMM for less. In order to fund this LUL had to make savings in three major areas. Optimisation of Current Operations was the first area. Current progress was such that in 1993/94 the company was in operating profit for the first time in its 130 year existence, but there was a limit to the savings that could be achieved without impacting operational capability. The second and third areas were Strategic Supplier Management and Innovative Engineering. This has involved working together with suppliers to capture the external technologies which can be brought to bear effectively inside LUL with an aim to reduce real costs (possibly through outsourcing).

The concurrence of the ADL and 'DMM for Less' visions was the driver which highlighted the need to work more closely with suppliers and forced supplier management up the LUL agenda. This has produced the supply chain schematic of figure 7.5.

FIGURE 7.5: SUPPLY CHAIN POST INTRODUCTION OF SUPPLIER MANAGERS

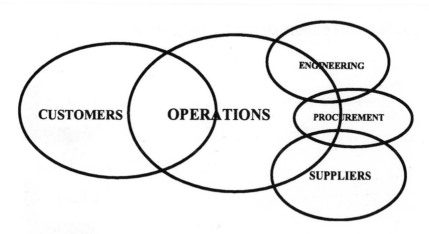

Making this vision a reality was a potential nightmare because many of the activities in the '7-box model' were totally unfamiliar to LUL staff, one of whom described it as 'looking into the abyss'. Allowing suppliers greater involvement in the operations of LUL was described as similar to inviting an unknown guest into your house. With 6000 active suppliers, how could LUL select the correct ones? It was necessary, first, to find a well researched and developed methodology which had been tried and tested in the real world. What was not wanted was glossy words, diagrams, or theory, without practical application. The situation was too important for LUL to be a test bed.

Following a search of the market place LUL selected the SCMG Ltd process.

Section 2 The SCMG Ltd Relationship Improvement Process

SCMG Ltd grew out of a series of research projects supported by the Science and Engineering Research Council and the DTI in 1987. Initially this work was to study best practice in customer-supplier relationships in Just-in-Time situations in Electronics and Mechanical Engineering. The original research developed a process of measuring inter-company relationships against a best practice model and associating the resultant continuous improvement process. This is called the Relationship

Positioning Tool (RPT) and forms essentially phase 4 and 5 of the Relationship Improvement Process (RIP) shown in figure 7.6.

FIGURE 7.6: THE RELATIONSHIP IMPROVEMENT PROCESS

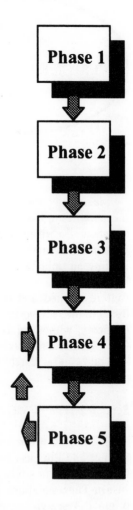

- **Phase 1:**
  - **Internal Commitment**
    & Team Building

- **Phase 2:**
  - **Partner Selection**

- **Phase 3:**
  - **Supplier Commitment**
    & Communication

- **Phase 4:**
  - **Relationship Measurement**
    & Analysis

- **Phase 5:**
  - **Action, Implementation**
    & Progress Review

The basic principle of the approach is to aid the move from adversarial to collaborative relationships as shown in figure 7.7.

FIGURE 7.7: ADVERSARIAL VERSUS COLLABORATIVE

✗   ✓

• Reactive	• ProActive
• Competitive	• Cooperative
• No-trust	• Trust Cooperative
• Frequent tendering	• Life contracts
• One way information	• Two way information
• Customer specification	• Joint design
• Sole investment risk	• Shared investment risk
• Supplier not seen as integral	• Suppliers seen as part of family
• Multi-sourcing	• Single sourcing
• Competitive tendering	• Joint benchmarking
• Stress imposed by customer	• Joint drive for excellence
• Benefit?	• Mutual benefit

The belief is that in 'pure' market situations, where price is the only differentiating factor, the adversarial win-lose situation can still apply. In most industrial transactions (and certainly in the LUL case) there is a history and an 'expectation' of future transactions which changes the game to one in which both parties can win. No one however should move to a Partnering or Partnership Sourcing (Macbeth and Ferguson 1994) approach unless there is a business benefit. The business case is the key determining factor.

LUL was, however, not ready to commit to the full 5 phase process. The initial project was directed at phases 1 and 2 primarily and, to a more limited extent, to phase 3. This process involved discussions with LUL to calibrate their selection criteria and to apply parts of the RPT, to create a more comprehensive definition of the criteria for supplier selection, consistent with the key LUL requirements. The criteria concentrated on aspects of current performance using the scales of Quality, Delivery, Cost and Innovation, as well as Supplier Capability and Information Flow. Workshops were held with LUL and supplier personnel to discuss the issues and results.

In the LUL environment the requirement to comply with EC Procurement Directives was also paramount. The process has been beneficial in supporting LUL in the implementation of its Supplier Management vision.

Section 3 Results and Future Development

As part of phase 1 and 2 of the process, internal workshops were held that produced a list of key capability criteria used in selecting suppliers and this is shown in Table 7.3. In similar fashion, the LUL commitment to suppliers was also identified and is listed in Table 7.4.

Table 7.3:   Key Criteria Relative to Capability used in Selecting Suppliers with whom Collaborative Relationships can be Formed to Achieve The Decently Modern Metro:

- **Interest in a long term relationship**
- **Willingness to invest and share risk**
- **Interest/experience in collaborative relationships**
- **Experience across industries and/or technologies**
- **R&D and design capability**
- **Sound skill base and training to maintain it**
- **Technical innovation/ability to reverse engineer**
- **Flexibility in manufacture**
- **Financially and managerially sound**

Table 7.4:   What London Underground Limited Must do to Attract and Interest Suppliers in Collaborative Relationships:

- **Provide long term commitment**
- **Offer bigger packages**
- **Share risk (and reward) and trust them**
- **Use more of their knowledge and experience**
- **Involve them more in decision making**
- **Discuss long term planning and total cost budgeting**
- **Define requirements in terms of quality, delivery and benefit**
- **Define the whole operating environment**
- **Avoid prescriptive bespoke specifications**
- **Allow input into specification, design and tender process**

The project also identified key issues and concerns with collaborative relationships (as shown in Table 7.5), and these will be examined closely as the overall implementation process continues. Major barriers to the change were identified during interactive workshop sessions and are listed in Table 7.6.

Table 7.5:   Key Issues and Concerns when Entering Into Collaborative Relationships

- **How do you build trust - how can you forget the past?**
- **Aligning missions and objectives**
- **Measuring joint performance and success, what are the tangible benefits**
- **How do you judge value for money and maintain competition**
- **Role of the contract - can you keep the lawyers out**
- **How do you cope with failure**
- **Equitable sharing of risk**

Table 7.6:   Barriers to Success in Implementing Collaborative Relationships

SOCIAL
- **natural competitiveness**
- **lack of trust in others**
- **fear of failure**
- **job preservation**

ATTITUDINAL
- **risk aversion**
- **short term profitism**
- **fear of loss of control**
- **lack of board commitment**

STRUCTURAL
- **too many levels**
- **rigid structures**
- **lack of empowerment**
- **unclear roles & responsibilities**

OPERATIONAL
- **lack of time to change**
- **over complex systems**
- **uncoordinated objectives**
- **withholding key information**

PROCEDURAL
- **too much audit and bureaucracy**
- **restrictive standing orders and EC legislation**
- **adversarial methods and forms of contracting**
- **over-prescription by customer**

The results have demonstrated the need to continue to develop the supplier management role and the magnitude of the task to understand and alter long standing confrontational and adversarial positions by both LUL and its supply base. New staff have been appointed and training by SCMG Ltd has commenced. A continuing relationship between LUL and SCMG Ltd is planned to transfer to LUL the capability to use SCMG tools and processes.

In each of these the intention is to create a collaborative relationship, bringing together the academic and commercial wings of SCMG Ltd with LUL to provide a practical 'test bench' for further projects. In this way the two organisations will be putting into practice the principles that LUL wishes to operate with their suppliers to deliver the supply chain of the future (See figure 7.8).

FIGURE 7.8: SUPPLY CHAIN OF THE FUTURE

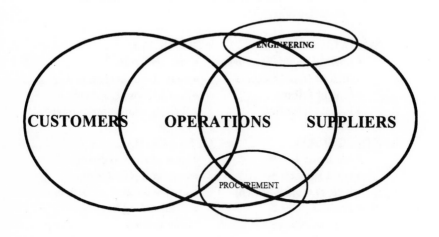

References

Hope, R. D. (1994) 'Decently Modern Metro still an elusive goal', *Railway Gazette*, 150 (1), pp. 41-44.

London Underground Ltd, (1991) Company Plan.

London Underground Ltd. (1994) Making a vision into reality.

Macbeth, D.K. and Ferguson, N. (1994) *Partnership Sourcing: an integrated supply chain approach*, London, FT/Pitman.

Millett, B. (1993/4) '*Customer first on hand on London Underground*', Trans Mechanical Engineering IE Australia, Volume ME19, No. 1, pp. 1-9

Monopolies & Mergers Commission (1991), London Underground Ltd, 'A report on passenger and other services supplied by the company', London, HMSO.

Public Enquiry Investigation into the King's Cross Underground Fire (the Fennell Report) 1988.

London Underground Regrets, *The Economist*, July 1 1989, pp. 23-24.

PART D:

NETWORK SOURCING

142

CHAPTER 8

NETWORK SOURCING: THE CONCEPT EXPLAINED

Peter Hines

Introduction and Subject Review

This chapter explores the possibility of creating relationships between companies that would gain advantage from vertical integration, whilst giving flexibility to market conditions. The strategic importance of buyers and suppliers working together within an ongoing relationship was, until recently, largely unnoticed by both practitioners and academics. The almost sole exception to this was the classic article on Vertical Quasi-Integration written in 1972 by Blois. It was not, however, until the 1980s that the true strategic value of buyer-supplier relationships was being discussed in any depth. One of the first to do this was the Industrial Marketing and Purchasing (IMP) Group (Ford, 1980).

A key text in the literature on strategic inter-company relationships was Beyond Negotiation by Carlisle and Parker (1989). This book moved the focus from a traditional "win-lose" relationship to a scenario where a "win-win" relationship can be created. The advantages of creating a win-win scenario (or purchasing partnership) have been summarised by Ellram (1991) and are reproduced in Figure 8.1. This partnership is defined by Ellram as "an agreement between a buyer and a seller that involves a commitment, over an extended time period, and includes the sharing of information along with a sharing of the risks and rewards of the relationship".

Further related developments are supply chain management (Macbeth et al 1989) and pipeline management (Farmer and Ploos van Amstel, 1990). Both of these concepts take the relationship further by linking end consumers and raw materials sources. Both concepts are primarily concerned with optimising the total value chain by creating, within each individual company, the correct work allocation and relationship type between raw material and end consumption. Sako (1992) brings together a number of different aspects of relationship strategy based on comparative research between Japan and the UK. The focus of her work revolves around trust and the achievement of mutual benefit through long term relationships.

Figure 8.1:   Potential Advantages from Japanese-Style Subcontracting

---

Management

1. Reduced supplier base is easier to manage.
2. Increased mutual dependence lowers risk of losing supply source and creates greater stability through increased supplier loyalty.
3. Reduced time looking for new suppliers/gathering competitive bids.
4. Allows for joint planning and information sharing based on mutual trust and benefit.
5. Loyalty may increase supplier attention and customer service in areas such as:
   • lead time reliability
   • Priority in times of scarcity
   • Increased attention when problems arise
6. Greater cooperation from suppliers to support the firm's strategy.

Technology

1. Partners may be more willing to share/give access to technology.
2. Partners may be more willing and capable of participating in product design based on knowledge and commitment to the other partner.
3. Supplier knowledge/involvement in design may:
   • Improve quality
   • Reduce time to market for new products/design changes

Financial

1. May share business risks through:
   • Joint investment
   • Joint research and development
   • Sharing of financial risks associated with market shifts
2. Information sharing/forecasting may reduce inventory levels.
3. Long-term commitment of a partnership may lead to more stable supply prices.

Source: Ellram (1991)

The most recent work on relationships is the Lean Supply model developed by Lamming (1993) in the context of his work in the International Motor Vehicle Programme (Womack et al, 1990). As indicated in Chapter 3, within the Lean Supply model, Lamming shows that it is not the individual abilities or strategies of buyers or sellers that are important; it is the mutual relationship between the two that is the key to their joint strategy.

The above authors have all made important contributions to the understanding of the buyer-supplier relationship but either fail to produce a coherent explanatory model or a practical implementation methodology. If work in this area is to be of practical use to companies and organisations it is important that both of these issues should be addressed. This chapter attempts to do this in conjunction with the accompanying chapter which shows how Calsonic Llanelli Radiators adopted such an approach.

Network Sourcing: A New Explanatory Model

The need for a new explanatory model is threefold:

- First, there are a number of common misconceptions about how the buyer-supplier relationship operates, particularly in Japan, leading to inaccurate academic texts and poor practitioner advice,

- Second, there is also a significant degree of misconception about the development of close buyer-supplier relations, particularly concerning the key explanatory factors related to relative causality, and

- Third, as noted above, a model linking existing practices at world class companies with a practical implementation route will assist practitioners in their improvement activities.

The Network Sourcing Model is based on the author's observations of how relationships between buyers and suppliers are undertaken at the world's best companies, particularly those in the Japanese automotive, electronics and capital equipment industries. It is contended that this network approach provides customers and sellers alike with considerable competitive advantage for their combined products.

The model is termed Network Sourcing because leading organisations are moving away from the traditional Japanese style subcontracting system, based on a simple tiered pyramid structure, to reliance on an extended network of direct and indirect suppliers. It is argued that this network is becoming the key to the competitive advantage of the final product. This viewpoint was first expounded by Professor Itsutomo Mitsui in 1991:

> *'The Japanese system of subcontracting is no longer the closed, highly integrated, pyramidal and hierarchical structure it used to be. The type of relationship and the forms of collaboration are diversifying. Before long the Japanese structure of subcontracting will have become an extensive network system...(The interests of the final assemblers) lie not in a relationship of dependence on a group of suppliers, but in the development of open and flexible (mutually dependent) networks.'*

The deliverables of Network Sourcing can be summarised as quality, cost, new product development and delivery.

There are ten major characteristics of the Japanese subcontracting system which are uniquely combined in this Network Sourcing model and, it can be argued, are key ingredients in the economic success of industrial Japan. These characteristics are summarised in Table 8.1 and will be individually discussed below. Before describing these features it should be stressed, however, that it is very difficult to isolate the relative importance of these individual factors; and indeed, it is their interaction that forms the unique Network Sourcing environment in Japan. A fuller discussion of these characteristics can be found in Hines 1994a.

a. Tiering Structure and Reliance on Small Firms

> *'Japan has twice as many small companies as the US - and nearly ten times as many as Britain. For the last 30 years, they have been the critical first stage of the economic rocket that has made Japan a by-word for industrial competition.'*
> C. Smith (1982)

Table 8.1: Network Sourcing Overview

---

a. A tiered supply structure with a heavy reliance on small firms.

b. A small number of direct suppliers with individual part numbers sourced from one supplier but within a competitive dual sourcing environment.

c. High degrees of asset specificity among suppliers and risk sharing between customer and supplier alike.

d. A maximum buy strategy by each company within the semi-permanent supplier network, but a maximum make strategy within these trusted networks.

e. A high degree of bilateral design employing the skills and knowledge of both customer and supplier alike.

f. A high degree of superior innovation in both new products and processes.

g. Close, long-term relations between network members involving a high level of trust, openness and profit sharing.

h. The use of rigorous supplier grading systems increasingly giving way to supplier self-certification.

i. A high level of supplier co-ordination by the customer company at each level of the tiered supply structure.

j. A significant effort made by customers at each of these levels to develop their suppliers.

The fundamental building blocks of Japan's manufacturing strength are its small and medium enterprises (SMEs). Whilst the percentage of establishments with less than 100 employees is similar in Japan and the UK (97.8% and 94.2%) for manufacturing companies, the employment profiles are quite different. In Japan firms with less than 100 people employ 56.7% of the total manufacturing employment: this figure is less than half (27.3%) in the UK. Although the value added per employee by these small companies is typically less than for larger companies, such small enterprises still represent a very significant portion of the Japanese manufacturing economy. Kinoshita (1986) has shown that small and medium businesses (with less than 300 employees) were responsible for 52% of the total manufacturing output in Japan. It follows that, unless these small companies show significant expertise in manufacturing, it would be impossible for the final assemblers (who perhaps add as little as 15 to 30% of the final product's value) to be world class.

The structure into which these Japanese SMEs fit has traditionally been seen as a tiered pyramid of the different levels of supply, with the final assembler sitting at the apex. These firms, such as Toyota, are supplied by first tier firms (typically employing 300 to 1000 employees) although there are a number of significantly larger firms, such as Nippondenso. In the automotive industry there may typically be around 200 to 300 such suppliers providing sub-assemblies or systems per final assembler.

The first tier companies are supplied by a larger number of second tier suppliers providing sub-assemblies, such as metal pressings. Each of the first tier firms has in the region of 25 to 30 of these second tier suppliers. The latter are typically small in size, employing 10 to 300 people. These second tier suppliers have their own subcontractors, who provide them with specialist process abilities such as plating, casting and machining. These third tier suppliers are normally very small, with fewer than 10 employees, and they are required to be extremely flexible in their work. Each second tier supplier may retain the services of 6 to 10 of these third tier firms. In some instances, particularly in the automotive industry, there may even be fourth and fifth tier subcontractors, depending on the type of product and specialism required.

Within the tiering structure it is the responsibility of the customer tier to organise, communicate with and nurture the level below. Thus, the assembler takes responsibility for the welfare of the first tier suppliers, the first tier take responsibility for the second tier firms, and so on down the hierarchy.

This traditional pyramidal structure is however based on a single company network of supply, which encompasses all the relevant tiers necessary to produce the end product. Nishiguchi (1987) has argued that the resulting formation was similar to a series of mountain peaks. He called this the Alps Structure (Figure 8.2). When this industry specific view is enlarged to include the wider economy then a true picture of interlocking supplier networks can be seen. A simplified form of this is also outlined in Figure 8.2. Within this scenario Nishiguchi's Alps Structure takes the form of a series of different peaks with heights. Thus, there may be more tiers of supply in one industry sector than another, as is typically the case when comparing the automotive with the electronics industry.

Figure 8.2:   The Alps Structure and the Interlocking Network Sourcing Model

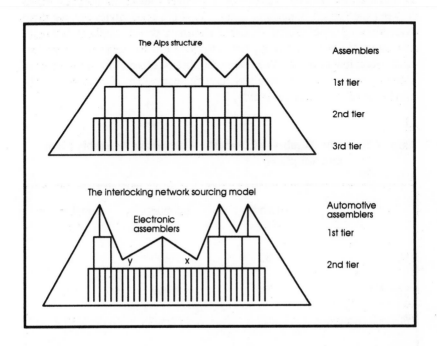

However, many of these firms supply more than one industry sector. This is particularly the case with electronics suppliers such as Hitachi. This is illustrated in Figure 8.2 where firms X and Y can be seen to supply both the automotive assemblers and the electronics assemblers. While X and Y have a direct, or first tier relationship with the electronics assembler illustrated, they are indirect suppliers to the automotive firms.

b. Few Supply Sources

Customers typically have few suppliers and therefore suppliers have few customers. This means that the number of intercompany linkages can be kept to an absolute minimum. As a result, a higher degree of manpower can be put into the formation, maintenance and improvement of each relationship.

The typical numbers of direct relationships within the automotive industry are far fewer than in the West. Table 8.2 shows how the number of relationships between automotive assembler and direct supplier varies between the United States and Japan. In the United States the big three assemblers all have several thousand domestic direct suppliers (although this figure has been somewhat reduced), whereas the Japanese assemblers have only a few hundred. Even when the data is adjusted for the number of assembly plants, the Japanese still have the equivalent of a quarter of the number of relationships per plant.

Table 8.2:   The Numbers of Domestic Automotive Assembly Plants and Suppliers

	Assembly Plants	Suppliers	Supplier per Plant
Ford	67	7,800	116
Chrysler	36	4,000	111
General Motors	147	12,500	85
Mazda	2	110	55
Honda	6	150	25
Toyota	11	250	22
Nissan	9	170	18

Source: Adapted from: Minato (1991)

The generally small number of direct contracts that assemblers have with their suppliers is mirrored in other Japanese sectors as well as the automotive sector. Table 8.3 shows that the number of suppliers is relatively constant between the general, electric, transport and precision machinery industries at between 200 and 300.

Table 8.3:   The Number of Suppliers used by Large Japanese Machinery Manufacturers

	1971	1981
General Machinery	253	291
Electric Machinery	278	222
Transport Machinery	288	244
Precision Machinery	189	251

Source: Adapted from: Minato (1991)

The relatively small number of customer-supplier contracts necessary has been cascaded down to the lower tiers in Japanese industry. For instance the number of direct contracts in the automotive industry was approximately 200 to 300 between assembler and first tier supplier, 25 to 30 between first tier and second tier, and 6 to 10 between subsequently lower tiers. As a result the degree of dependence by suppliers on customers for the percentage of the supplier's turnover rises the lower the tier of supply. Indeed, according to data from Japan's MITI, 64% of SME subcontractors have less than five customers. This enables them to pay close attention to their customers' requirements as well as minimising the amount of time they have to spend visiting a large customer base.

The obvious conclusion to this is that Japanese customers have fewer sources (probably only one) for each part that they buy. This is certainly the impression that Western firms have of the Japanese. However, this conclusion is presumptuous, certainly for the automotive industry, and almost certainly for other discrete Japanese industries as well. This is borne out by reference to Table 8.7 at the end of the chapter. It can be seen from the table that only 12% of parts are single sourced by automotive assemblers in Japan, compared to 69% by American firms based in the USA and 33% for European based firms.

Womack, Jones and Roos (1990) note that:

> *'Although many observers have argued that single-sourcing is another useful technique Western assemblers can learn from the Japanese, we've already seen that this argument is both wrong and beside the point. These same observers assumed that single sourcing in Japan led to longer-term relationships with suppliers. In fact, as we saw, Japanese long-term relationships do not depend on single-sourcing but on a contract framework that encourages co-operation.'*

The confusion over Japanese single sourcing has therefore arisen due to a misunderstanding of their hybrid system. This system exhibits some elements of single sourcing and some elements of dual sourcing. It is usually the case that a customer will have a number of actual (or potential) suppliers for a particular type of part, such as a car seat; although any particular seat (i.e. part number) will be ordered from only one supplier, who in almost all cases would be awarded the business for the lifetime of the part number.

This hybrid sourcing is of major importance as it not only allows for a high degree of competition for new part numbers when a new car model is announced, but it allows for all the benefits of single sourcing within the period of manufacture. It should also be noted that the competing suppliers for any one part number would all be members of the customer's network of long term supply. Losing the business for a new bumper, for instance, does not mean, therefore, that the supplier will not win the business for future part numbers.

Such a system acts to the benefit of the suppliers, the customer and the ultimate consumer because it creates and maintains intense competition within the supplier network. This overcomes a major potential problem with single sourcing while also allowing very close partnership style relationships to be maintained with all suppliers. This system also helps to facilitate inter-company problem solving and to create an atmosphere where continual improvement (or Kaizen) can flourish. A more detailed discussion of this hybrid sourcing model can be found in Hines 1994b.

c. Asset Specificity and Risk Sharing

Asset specificity is concerned with the degree to which suppliers make specific investments concerned with their ability to supply any one particular customer. In general, the greater the degree of specificity of an investment to any one customer, the greater the degree of risk sharing in new projects, but also the greater potential that exists for short-term opportunism and blackmailing by either trading partner. As Sako (1993) explains:

> *'After the supplier undertakes such investment, it might refuse production and delivery unless higher prices are offered. The customer might equally threaten to cancel orders without compensation (leaving the supplier to bear the sunk cost) for the purpose of extracting lower prices.'*

Thus, for a high degree of asset specificity to exist there must already be a high degree of trust between the partners, based on the expectation that they will not seek short-term gains at the expense of their partner and that there will be a shared mutual gain. This is reinforced when there is an expectation of long-term relationships and hence lower risks of asset specific investments. The key is, therefore, trust between the two parties, which is largely formed by a history of positive actions in the past engendered within a positive environment.

There are four important types of asset specificity: these are, respectively: physical, dedicated, human and site. These will be discussed using comparative evidence drawn from Nishiguchi (1989, 1994) (Table 8.4).

Physical and dedicated asset specificity consists of the degree to which mobile and physical features (such as specific dies, moulds and tooling for the manufacture of customer specific products) are invested in by the subcontractor. Dedicated asset specificity, in contrast, is the degree to which discrete and/or additional investment in production capacity is made by the subcontractor in the expectation of significant sales of product to a particular customer. Thus, physical asset specificity is concerned with customer specific moveable assets, whereas dedicated asset specificity is concerned with customer specific immovable assets.

Table 8.4:   Factored Asset Specificity Scored Between Tiers in the Japanese Electronic Industry

Asset Specificity	FACTOR SCORE			
	Japan		**UK**	
	Assembler — 1st Tier	1st Tier — 2nd Tier	Assembler — 1st Tier	1st Tier — 2nd Tier
Physical/ Dedicated	354 [*1]	296 [*1]	248 [*1]	235 [*1]
Human	6.9% [*2]	64.5% [*2]	3.4% [*2]	-
Site	100km [*3]	31km [*3]	79km [*3]	-

[*1]   Range 100-500. The higher the score the more physical and dedicated asset specific the subcontracting relation.

[*2]   Percentage of a subcontractors' employees per regular customer in the formers' total workforce.

[*3]   Kilometres between the subcontractor and its major customer defined as number 1 customer by sales value.

Source: Adapted from: Nishiguchi (1989)

Table 8.4 shows a summary of Nishiguchi's findings about the relationships between final assemblers and first tier suppliers (6 in Japan, 2 in the UK) and between first tier suppliers and second tier suppliers (24 in

Japan and 9 in the UK). In the UK there is a generally lower degree of asset specificity. There appears also to be little difference in the degree of specificity between assembler and the first tier on the one hand, and between the first tier and second tier on the other. Within the first to second tier relations in the UK there also seems to be little difference in the degree of specificity between subcontracting of a high technology nature and subcontracting of an assembly nature.

In contrast, physical and dedicated asset specificity appears to vary considerably in Japan, both between tiers, and by the type of subcontracting. The degree of asset specificity between assembler and first tier is significantly higher than that between first tier and second tier. Within the first to second tier relations in Japan there is also a considerably higher degree of these types of asset specificity between high technology and assembly subcontracting, with the latter showing a higher specificity.

Human asset specificity is concerned with the degree to which employees in subcontracting companies are educated and trained specifically to fulfil the requirements of one particular customer. This usually arises in a learning by doing situation, and is associated with long standing customer specific operations on dedicated equipment using dies, moulds and tooling.

In order to calculate the degree of human asset specificity in his sample Nishiguchi used the proxy of dividing the number of employees at subcontractors by the number of regular customers. This was then adjusted to take account of differences in the size of firms. The degree of human asset specificity in Japanese second tier subcontractors (at 64.5%) is extremely high, and is a clear consequence of the very limited customer base of such companies. The degree of human asset specificity is considerably lower in the first tier subcontractors. However, even at this level a near 30% ratio is recorded for first tier assembly subcontractors. The relative scores for the UK are considerably lower, although only first tier data is available. At this level the human asset specificity ratio is as low as 3.4% with little difference between high technology subcontractors and assembly subcontractors. It may be supposed that the degree of human asset specificity is higher than this in second tier UK subcontractors (perhaps between 10 and 30%) but it is still likely to be considerably less than the Japanese second tier figure.

Site asset specificity is the degree to which the separate manufacturing sites, responsible for the transformation of raw materials into finished products are located proximate to one another, so as to economise on the inventory and transportation expenses incurred as a result of their separate locations. In general, the greater the degree of site asset specificity (i.e. proximity) the lower are the chances that short term opportunism will be exhibited by either customer or supplier.

The aggregate data in Table 8.4 would suggest that the site asset specificity is lower in Japan than in the UK. However, two factors should be borne in mind. Firstly, Japan has a far larger land area and the centres of population are dispersed along the coastal plains. Secondly, during the 1960s, rural areas (such as Tohoku and Shinshu) away from the centres of manufacturing assembly, were used for electronics sub-assembly. As a result, first tier assemblers are not necessarily near their customers.

This fact is reflected in data which shows that Japanese first tier high technology firms (not employing cheap rural female labour) are only half the distance away from their customers, whereas first tier assemblers (using cheap rural female labour) are twice as far from their customers as in the UK. The distances between Japanese first tier assemblers and their second tier sub-assemblers, however, is very short. This is a reflection of second tier assembly taking place in rural districts to reduce labour costs, as well as due to a desire to be as close as possible to their customers.

In the UK the Japanese pattern of rural assemblers and clustered high technology firms seem to be absent. As a general reflection of the low customer concentration ratios, the benefits from setting up near any one particular customer are obviously reduced. As a result customers are scattered over a wide geographical area. Indeed, Nishiguchi found that several high technology subcontractors were in fact operating on a nationwide basis from one site.

Taking the four asset specificities together it is clear that the degree of asset specificity, certainly in the electronics industry, is higher in Japan than in the UK. This high asset specificity is a consequence of the existing close and trusting relationship between buyer and seller, rather than a cause of it. As a result, Japanese subcontractors can be seen to be highly customer focused and this allows them to reap benefits created by their close knowledge and understanding of their customers. This high degree of asset specificity also means that the risks associated with new product introduction are more equally balanced between customer and supplier in Japan than in the West.

d. Value Added Ratios

The degree of value adding within companies is low in Japan, both at the final assembly stage and at all tiers in the supplier network, but the loyalty to long term sources is high. On this point, Bruck (1988) concludes:

> *'The individual participant in an excellent network enacts a maximum-buy strategy while the whole network pursues a maximum-make strategy.'*

As a result of this, the value-added ratios are low by Western standards for a whole range of industries. Toyota, for instance, only accounts for 27% of the total costs of materials, tools and finished parts required to build their final products. General Motors in comparison is responsible for nearer 70% of the costs of their final products. Table 8.5, with data from all Japanese and the US supply tiers, shows that this type of difference is not just between the final assembler and the first tier supplier, but is the norm for the complete supplier network. In addition, the table shows that this comparatively low value-adding is common to the other discrete Japanese industries listed.

Table 8.5: Value Added Ratio in Japan and the United States

	US %	Japan %	Gap %
Manufacturing Average	42.0	33.1	8.9
General Machinery	54.4	42.3	12.1
Electric Machinery	57.2	38.4	18.8
Transport Machinery	42.2	26.6	15.6
Precision Machinery	65.0	40.6	24.4

Source: Adapted from: Minato (1991)

The overall gap between the manufacturing industry value-added in the United States and that in Japan is 8.9%. This figure includes all industries and also data from non-discrete parts industries, as well as from discrete parts industries. When data from some of Japan's most successful discrete parts industries is considered the value-adding gap between America and Japan widens considerably. Thus, in the general machinery industry it is 12%, in transport machinery 15%, in electric machinery 18% and in precision machinery 24%. In the light of these gaps the degree of value adding in non-discrete parts industries must be very low or even nil. It should be noted that it is the discrete parts industries, with these low value adding ratios, that are the heart of Japan's manufacturing success. It is, therefore, possible to conclude that the importance of the supplier network for deliveries is far greater in Japan than in the West, particularly in the discrete parts industries.

An example of the lower value adding ratios can be seen by comparing the way that colour televisions were produced in Japan and the UK as shown in Figure 8.3. In the UK case, the television manufacturer was responsible for final assembly, as well as a range of sub-assembly tasks, such as PC boards and cabinet assemblies. Indeed, the UK manufacturer may even have been responsible for manufacturing some single parts such as plastic mouldings. The purchase of supplies in the UK case was divided between subcontracted (customer unique) parts and purchased (common to other customers) parts. It should be noted that the percentage of subcontracted parts was very low and normally limited to simple side operations, often taking advantage of cheaper labour outside of the main manufacturer. Such operations might include the cutting of lead lines, the removal of terminal film and the packing of instruction booklets in plastic bags.

In contrast Japanese colour television manufacturers have traditionally had a very different make or buy ratio. There is, in Japan, a considerably higher 'bought in' content and, consequently lower in-house value adding ratio. The Japanese manufacturer is much more likely to be an assembler of the end product. Indeed, in many cases, particularly for older models, even this task is subcontracted to subcontractors. The level of standard products purchased is similar in both countries. The Japanese manufacturer, however, may be able to purchase some standard cabinet bodies and some PC boards rather than making these products in-house, as was normally the case in the UK.

Figure 8.3: The Production Structures for the Manufacture of Colour Television in Japan and the UK

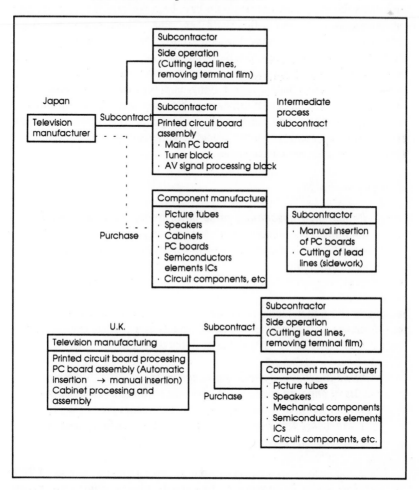

The big difference between the two countries has been in the subcontracting of special parts. The first noteworthy feature is that a far greater proportion of parts were subcontracted. In addition to employing subcontracting for simple parts with low labour costs, as occurs in the UK, Japanese firms also buy in more technical parts. These technical parts include the main PC boards, the tuner blocks and the AV signal processing blocks, all of which are made in-house in the UK. The second noteworthy feature in Japan is that second tier subcontractors are also employed. In such cases the value adding that might have been performed by the first tier subcontractors is divided with second tier firms. These second tier firms provide services such as manual insertion on PC boards, as well as some of the simpler subcontracting tasks, like lead line cutting. In this way some of the work traditionally carried out in-house by UK manufacturers is spread across three firms in Japan, each relying on a very low value added ratio. As a result, a method for co-ordinating this extended supplier network is required, to ensure that each additional supply link does not cause excessive diseconomies which would counterbalance the benefits of specialisation and core competencies.

e. Bilateral Design

> *'Rather than negotiating price downstream, customers and subcontractors alike began step by step to look at the possibility of reducing costs at the source by means of joint problem solving.'*
>
> *(Nishiguchi, 1989)*

One of the major methods to achieve joint problem solving is through the development of consumer focused products at a higher level of quality and at lower cost. Thus, as Nishiguchi elaborates:

> *'In addition to VA techniques that were useful in reducing costs of ongoing components while maintaining or enhancing product quality, value engineering (VE) techniques came to be widely used at the design stage in order to reduce costs of new products.'*

It became clear that, because subcontractors supplied in excess of 70% of the value of the end products, they should play a major role in new product development. Suppliers in Japan have, therefore, become greatly involved in what has become known as bilateral design. Table 8.1 summarises the involvement of suppliers in this shared design in the automotive industry. In the Japanese case, suppliers have a much greater responsibility for the design effort in terms of engineering time input than their customers. In the United States, however, the suppliers input is merely 14% of the total with European suppliers occupying an intermediary position in this regard.

The move from unilateral (customer specified design) to bilateral design has opened up major opportunities for suppliers to assist their customers, not only as a result of their design input but also in the area of design for manufacturability. It was of course almost impossible for customers to be able to design products that other companies were supposed to make. The chances of effective design co-ordination between the manufacturing and engineering staff and the supplier is obviously increased when design is undertaken at the supplier's premises.

Data in Table 8.7 shows that the role of the supplier outside Japan is primarily in assembler designed parts, with these representing 81% and 54% of the total respectively in America and Europe. The Japanese, however, exhibit a much lower degree of assembler designed parts in their cars (30%). The largest share of parts in the Japanese case (62%) are so called black box parts. This compares with 16% and 39% in America and Europe respectively. The final category of parts shown in Table 8.7 are supplier proprietary parts, which represent 8% of the total in Japan, 3% in America and 7% in Europe. If data for the European specialist luxury sector is stripped however (as this sector was very small in Japan in the late 1980s when the data was assembled) the figure for Europe rises to 10%.

The key to bilateral design is the early involvement of the subcontractor in the new product development process. A generic model of this earlier involvement is shown in Figure 8.4. The starting point for new product development is that three major inputs are made from both customer and supplier alike. These are inputs relating to a value analysis of existing products, suggestions on process improvements in the manufacture of existing products and a detailed analysis of competitors' products and processes at a customer and supplier level. At the concept stage the design function plays the key role in ensuring the total design of the complete product, be it a car, a television or a washing machine. The coordination of the different inputs, be they individual parts, sub-assemblies or systems, is done always by the customer. All subsequent requirements flow from this even though the suppliers have had three major inputs before this stage.

**Figure 8.4:   Generic Model Showing Early Involvement of Suppliers
in the New Product Development Process in Japan**

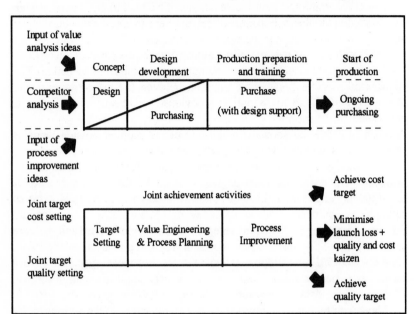

In the design development stage suppliers have a larger role than the customer company. It is the role of the customer's purchasing department to coordinate design development work with relevant suppliers. This is usually achieved bilaterally, with both the customer's designers and those of the supplier involved. As a result there is a split responsibility between design and purchasing. After this, and during the production preparation and trailing stages, the supplier takes over almost full responsibility for the project, although coordination is offered by the customer's purchasing department. At the start of production the customer will undertake to purchase parts for the life of the product.

Running in parallel with this design cycle are two important targeting processes: the first is the targeting of cost and the second is the targeting of quality. At the very first stages of involvement, cost and quality targets are set jointly between customer and supplier for those parts for which a particular supplier is to furnish. These targets are a response to end customer demands, and are generally set during the concept development stage. During the design development stage the key between customer and supplier is through value engineering and process planning, to ensure that quality and cost targets are brought within reach. Typically at this stage the product may be within 5% of its target cost, but may still require significant efforts to meet its quality targets.

The final achievement of quality and cost targets occurs during the production preparation and trailing stages when process improvements are made to the product when manufactured, using Industrial Engineering techniques. At the start of the production stage target quality and cost should be achieved. It is, then, the responsibility of the supplier to minimise any launch loss and disruption and, subsequently, to seek kaizen improvements in quality and cost.

f. Supplier Innovation

As a result of this bilateral design process Womack et al (1990) note that:

> *'Japanese assemblers gain from the increasing willingness of their suppliers to come up with innovations and cost saving suggestions and to work collaboratively. The system replaces a vicious circle of mistrust with a virtuous circle of cooperation.'*

This virtuous circle of cooperation can lead to increasing levels of supplier innovation. Over time, in Japan, black box designs have become the most common type of product supplied in the automotive industry. Customers are responsible for providing only a basic size and shape outline, with performance specifications. The supplier increasingly takes responsibility for the details of the sub-assembly (or part making) by the use of expertise and specialist knowledge. This development has meant that supplier competition has started to be based on technology competencies. This type of black box system of design additionally gives suppliers a major incentive to propose new ideas, to invest and, consequently, to expand their businesses. This is in contrast to the Western system by which supply drawings to suppliers who have little potential or incentive to innovate. In this way the Japanese have managed to unlock some mutualy competitive advantages within their suppliers, resulting in increased sales of lower cost and better quality products.

Due to the resulting trend towards large variety, small lot production and shortened product life cycles, there has been a strong stimulus for R & D orientated firms capable of developing their own products rather than simply relying on their customer for design drawings. In addition, such firms are increasingly becoming involved in designing for production of end parts even when this is undertaken by another company.

g. Relationship Type

> *'(The Japanese subcontracting system) implements coherently and simultaneously the fundamentals of Japanese management through the industrial structure, from the biggest to the smallest production units, founding competitivity on the rationality of cooperation, dependence being reciprocal, not only in theory, but (also) in practice.'*

> *Bruck (1988)*

This Japanese system can, it is argued here, be best characterised by the term Network Sourcing. This concept implies long-term relationships in which mutual trust, cooperation and clearly defined responsibilities are established. The system usually contains formal contracts between firms, but these encompass only rough guidelines for the relationship in the very broadest of terms. One of these contracts would typically contain very general information about the type of parts (e.g. metal pressings) the supplier is to deliver. There would rarely be any specific details about price, quality and delivery quantities. This type of information, which is the key to the successful relationship, would be informally agreed, based on a trusting relationship. In Japan, to have recourse to a formal contract would involve considerable loss of face to both parties and is, consequently, extremely rare practice.

Within these relationships, Lamming (1993) correctly identifies that the level of pressure between customer and supplier is very high. The closeness of the relations and the sharing of objectives should not be confused with a cosy relationship where there is an absence of pressure. This very high level of pressure is maintained partly by the use of multiple sourcing of component types as outlined above. The setting of stringent targets, in terms of quality and cost, are not completely imposed by customers but are the result of joint discussion and agreement. Indeed, allowing suppliers to have a major role in setting the targets ensures that they are often far more severe than if the customer had set them alone. Such targets are also more likely to be realistic and owned by the supplier than under adversarial contracting.

Another manifestation of the closeness of the relationship is the fact that there is often a degree of shared ownership between customer and supplier. The customer often takes a part share in the supplier's capital equity.

The pursuit of long-term relations is another major feature of Network Sourcing. The desire for long-term relations is not only sought by the supplier but also by the customer, who invests: effort in forming, coordinating and improving the relationship; time in the development of the supplier; and money in terms of loans or equity.

A survey into Japanese trading relations in 1987 by Sako (1992) found that, of the 2241 large companies who responded, 61% said that almost all transactions are long-term and have been continuous for at least 5 years, whilst 37% said that a significant majority of transactions are of this type. The remaining 2%, although not stated, are not believed to maintain long-term relations with suppliers. The most important reasons cited for maintaining these long-term relations were:

88%   Stable Supply
73%   Good Quality
50%   Competitive Price
48%   Trusting Relations as a Result of Long-Term Trading

It should be noted that less than 6% said that membership of a vertical *Keiretsu* was a reason. Thus, it would appear that these relations are long-term because it is economically viable for both parties to maintain such relations. One of the major reasons would appear to be that neither customers nor suppliers have to go through the time consuming and wasteful process of getting to know each other, due to frequently changing short-term, supply arrangements.

The Japanese Network Sourcing environment is characterised by a high degree of inter-company trust. Sako (1992) has classified this trust into three types:

1. Contractual Trust: The mutual expectation that promises of a written or verbal nature will be kept,

2. Competence Trust: The confidence that a trading partner is
                                    competent to carry out a specific task, and

3. Goodwill Trust: Commitments from both parties that they
                                    will do more than is formally required.

Within Network Sourcing each of these types of trust is present and, consequently, much inter-company waste is removed. The point here is that the Western convention of inspecting goods as they arrive means there is a lack of trust in the abilities of the supplier (competence trust), or in their good intentions (contractual trust). Problems in the quality of supplied goods would normally fall into the former category. However, in Japan, goods inward inspection has become less common because suppliers are trusted, not only to be competent, but to stick to their side of the (often unwritten) bargain. It is also important to note that, as there is an increasing trend towards greater subcontracting of goods and design in Japan, the customer is increasingly less able to control the supplier, and must, therefore, rely to an even greater extent on competence trust in both of these areas.

The three types of trust are obviously interlinked but the last, goodwill trust, cannot occur if the former two are not present. Sako again explains:

> *'What distinguishes 'goodwill trust' from 'contractual trust'*
> *is the expectation in the former case that trading partners*
> *are committed to take initiatives (or exercise discretion) to*
> *exploit new opportunities over and above what was explicitly*
> *promised.'*

The key here is that trading partners are not only pursuing their own interests, but are also seeking to offer their trading partner a competitive advantage, even at a slight cost to themselves. If both partners do the same then the combined efforts of both customer and supplier will lead to a joint competitive advantage, which will obviously help in selling their collective product to the end consumer. In the Network Sourcing System this type of mutual dependency is exactly the type of relationship that both buyer and supplier seek to maintain.

h. Supplier Grading and Self Certification

Supplier grading became a widespread practice in the 1960s in Japan. This occurred at the same time as suppliers were being organised into *Kyoryoku kai* associations. The grading mechanism was one of the chosen methods to institutionalise competition. Grading in its widest sense usually involved some measurement of product quality, price, delivery performance and engineering and technology performance. Each of these indicators was scored. A typical scoring scheme (such as the one used by Fuji Electric) would give 20 points each for quality, price and delivery, with 15 points each for management competence and long-term business viability, and 10 points for other special factors. As a result each subcontractor was given a grade: A for 80-100, B for 65-79, C for 50-64, D for 30-49 and E for less than 30.

Individual subcontractors would each be given the full results of their scores, perhaps on a three-monthly basis. They would also be informed of their standing in relation to other suppliers as well as being given an indication of weak points for improvement. This improvement would often take the form of joint action by both the customer and the supplier. In addition to this the names and details of the supplier were also displayed on purchasing department noticeboards in areas frequented by suppliers. This public display generally related only to quality and delivery performance data, with red circles made around particularly bad scores. Such data was typically updated on a monthly basis.

In this way intense competition was created amongst suppliers for a high place. This provided a major incentive for a continuous improvement because suppliers achieving the best scores, or rapid improvements, would be rewarded under the dual product sourcing/single part number sourcing policy. The other side of this was that poor performance would be punished with reduced business opportunities but with continual assistance to ensure that this position was only temporary. Suppliers were rarely discarded as a result of poor performance, certainly not until both customer and supplier had done everything within their powers to try to correct the situation. A more typical scenario was for the less able subcontractors to take a lower tier position in the supplier network, such as in the second or even third tier. This grading also meant that competition was not only against competitors (inside and outside the customer's network of supply) but between the different suppliers, which further improved performance.

The above discussion has been written in the past tense because grading systems by the best customers have recently become less comprehensive and of less importance (Lamming, 1993). The reason for this is that, as the performance of subcontractors improved between 1960 and the 1980s. 100% quality and delivery performance started to become the norm. Reporting on these features, therefore, started to become a non-value adding activity and was hence reduced or discontinued. Thus the responsibility for delivery and, particularly, quality was given to the supplier. This is another instance where the level of competence trust has increased tremendously in Japanese inter-company relationships.

i. Supplier Coordination

It is apparent from the foregoing discussions that the Japanese system of Network Sourcing has many advantages. This system did not, however, occur overnight, nor did it occur without significant efforts from both customers and suppliers alike. The key to its success comes through coordination and the development of methods which until very recently were uniquely deployed in Japan.

This coordination involves, as Norman (1991) puts it:

> *'(The) mutual involvement of the firms in the various tiers*
> *aimed at improving design, quality and efficiency. There is a*
> *remarkable source of dynamic cost advantage that flows*
> *from this mutual involvement. It is based upon constant two-*
> *way flows of strategic information between suppliers and*
> *buyers of the components and products. The aim is to seek*
> *ongoing technological improvements (kaizen) by the active*
> *use of the systems of JIT and TQC at every layer in the*
> *subcontracting pyramid.'*

The primary mechanism by which this has been achieved is the *kyoryoku kai* which literally means cooperative circle (although the term Supplier Association has been used by the author). It has many similarities with the internal quality circles adopted by many Western companies in the 1980s. In common with these quality circles there is a severe danger of failure when *kyoryoku kai* is copied in the West, unless great care is taken to translate both the benefit as well as the considerable effort which is necessary on the part of the buyer and seller alike. It is all too easy to look at the benefits and then wonder why things have not worked only in practice.

These *kyoryoku kai* can be viewed as communication, coordination and development tools that have resulted in the deployment of successful Japanese management and manufacturing techniques, throughout the complete network of supply over a period of several decades. Within the automotive industry these Supplier Associations have been gradually cascading down the tiering structure so that the benefits outlined above are now enjoyed by lower tier companies. As a result of this within the Japanese automotive industry, final assemblers managed to achieve significant competitive advantages by unlocking hidden potentials for mutual advantage in all the layers of the Supplier Network. These *kyoryoku kai* have now spread to other sectors, particularly in the discrete parts industries.

j. Supplier Development

The role of supplier development in Network Sourcing is crucial and it is through technology transfer investment by customer firms that subcontractors are able to reach the levels of excellence commonly experienced in Japan today. This investment involves both the transfer of hard technologies as well as softer management technologies. The flow of information has largely been within *kyoryoku kai* groupings and was, initially, almost exclusively from customer to subcontractor. Over time the transfer of knowledge has involved the active development of transfer of subcontractors by same tier subcontractors, the development of second tier subcontractors to their customers. It is obvious that this mutual assistance could only take place within an environment of extremely high goodwill trust, not only between buyer and supplier, but also between all the firms in the final assembler's network of supply.

This type of trust was primarily developed by the widespread adoption of *kyoryoku kai* throughout networks. These associations not only helped form joint strategies and gave development help to suppliers en masse, but also created the necessary trust so that one-to-one supplier activities could be achieved. The aim of these activities are normally joint problem solving and continual improvement.

A Review of Causality

In reviewing the way that UK firms have approached the creation of close
or partnership style relationships it has become clear that, in many cases,
there is little attempt by firms to put in the necessary hard work over a
period of time to create a firm bedrock upon which a lasting relationship
can be built. In far too many cases the buyer and supplier 'partners' decide
that they now have a partnership and attempt to cherry pick the best parts
of the Network Sourcing model without really changing the underlying
relationship.

Figure 8.5: Major Causal Relationships Within Network Sourcing

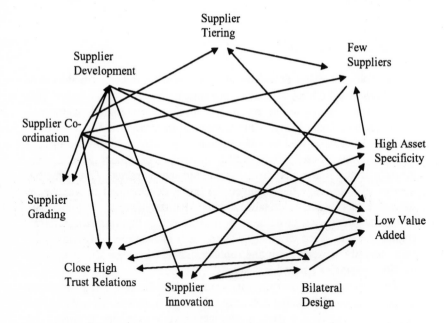

As a result of this major shortcoming in how 'partnerships' are formed
this section reviews the interactions between the different elements of
Network Sourcing, on the basis of detailed observations in Japan about how
these relationships are formed. Figure 8.5 demonstrates how the major
causality flows operate between the ten key characteristics of the Network

Sourcing model. As can be seen from this model there are a range of causality flows:

- where causality flows from one characteristic to another without a corresponding reverse flow,

- where causality flows from one characteristic to another with an equal and opposite flow, and

- where there is little or no apparent causality flow.

Analysis of these major flows shows that there are 21 of the first type of causality flow, two of the second type, with the remainder being of the third type. It is therefore apparent that where there is a causal inter-relationship, in almost all cases the causality is uni-directional. The two cases where this does not apply are between:

- 'High Asset Specificity' and 'Close High Trust Relations'; and,

- 'Low Value Added' and 'Supplier Tiering'.

In these two cases each factor has an equal and opposite causal relationship over the other. As noted above, however, in the vast majority of cases where there is a major causal relationships, the causation flows in only one direction. As an example, 'Supplier Development' can be clearly seen to influence 'Supplier's Innovative ability' positively but 'Supplier Innovation' has no effect on 'Supplier Development' activities.

In order to extend and clarify these causal flows, a Network Sourcing Causality Matrix has been developed (Figure 8.6). In this figure the causalities between each characteristic are displayed in a simple matrix format. Thus the first row of the diagram 'Supplier Tiering' describes which of the other characteristics has a causal effect upon Supplier Tiering. A major causality can be observed from both 'Low Added Value Ratio' and 'Supplier Coordination'. The effect on each variable from other variables is similarly displayed by reference to the row adjacent to the characteristic under consideration.

Figure 8.6: A Network Sourcing Causality Matrix

A \ B	Supplier Tiering	Few Suppliers	High Asset Specificity	Low Value Added Ratio	Bilateral Design	Supplier Innovation	Close High Trust Relations	Supplier Grading	Supplier Coordination	Supplier Development	Factor A affected by sum of Factor Bs — Effect Score	C/E Score — Cause/Effect Score
Supplier Tiering		O		●		O	O		●	O	10	(2)
Few Suppliers	●		●		O			O	●	O	12	(4)
High Asset Specificity	O	O			●	O	●		O		13	(4)
Low Value Added	●				●	●	O	O	●	●	17	(7)
Bilateral Design		O	O	O		●	O	O	●	O	12	0
Supplier Innovation		●	O	O	O		O		O	●	11	(2)
Close High Trust Relations	O	O	●	●	●	O		O	●	●	19	(10)
Supplier Grading							O		●	●	7	(2)
Supplier Coordination				O	O						2	21
Supplier Development		O	O	O			O	O	●		8	10
Factor B affects sum of Factor As — CAUSE SCORE	8	8	9	10	12	9	9	5	23	18		

Major causality flows are indicated by a black circle, minor causality flows are shown with a white circle. As a result it is possible to show that Supplier Tiering is caused to a limited degree by Few Suppliers as well as by a number of other variables.

The next stage of the analysis seeks to put a weighting against these strong and weak causation flows. In the case of a strong cause, 3 points are given and, in the case of weak flow, 1 point is awarded. As a result it is possible to estimate the total degree to which any one factor is affected by the sum of the other factors. Thus for 'Supplier Tiering', with 2 strong causes (2x3 points) and 4 weak causes (4x1), a total measure of the degree to which it is affected by all other factors is 10 points.

In a similar way it is possible to estimate the total degree to which one independent variable influences other, dependent variables. This is done by summing the scores in a column. Thus for the column adjacent to 'Supplier Tiering', with 2 strong causes (2x3 points) and 2 weak causes

(2x1), a total measure of the degree to which it effects other factors is 8 points. A similar analysis of effects and causes has been undertaken, and is summarised in the column and row respectively marked Effect Score and Cause Score.

In order to find out which characteristics are net causes and which are net effects it is possible to deduct the effect score from the cause score. This net score is depicted in the last column of the table labelled Cause/Effect Score (C/E Score). In order to clarify these net points scores this summary information has been portrayed in Table 8.6.

Table 8.6: Network Sourcing Causality Scores

Cause	C/E Score	
Supplier Coordination	21	PRIMARILY
Supplier Development	10	CAUSES
Bilateral Design	0	
Supplier Innovation	(2)	MIXED
Supplier Tiering	(2)	CAUSE
Supplier Grading	(2)	AND
High Asset Specificity	(4)	EFFECT
Few Suppliers	(4)	
Low Added Value Ratio	(7)	PRIMARILY
Close High Trust Relations	(10)	EFFECTS

Although care obviously needs to be taken when drawing inferences from this analysis, especially when discussing minor points differences, a clustering of the net scores reveals that there are three clearly definable types of characteristics within Network Sourcing:

• Variables that are primarily causes,

• Variables that are primarily effects, and

- Variables that have a largely mixed cause and effect although with the effect possibly slightly more important than the cause.

There are two characteristics which can be seen to be overwhelmingly causal variables, namely, 'Supplier Coordination' and 'Supplier Development'. Even allowing for the degree of subjectivity in the analysis it is clear that 'Supplier Coordination' is far and away the major causal variable, but 'Supplier Development' also plays an important role. These two areas, involving considerable investment in time and effort, particularly on the part of the customer, are crucially important for success. In addition when present within Network Sourcing they are a clear sign from customer to supplier that the former is 'investing' in the supplier, with a view to repayment with future reduced inter-company (buyer-supplier) and intra-company (supplier) waste.

The second clustering of variables are 'Low Added Value Ratio' and 'Close High Trust Relations', both of which can be seen to be primarily effects of other variables. It is interesting to note that these **effect** characteristics are the very ones most frequently chosen by UK companies wishing to implement, or cause, a 'partnership' style relationship. Without the input of causal variables however, a large percentage of these buyer-supplier 'partnerships' in the UK may become little more than cosmetic window dressing.

The third cluster of variables are those which are a mix of cause and effect. These characteristics are: 'Bilateral Design', 'Supplier Innovation', 'Supplier Tiering', 'Supplier Grading', 'High Asset Specificity' and 'Few Suppliers'. In the light of the relatively small points difference between these factors it would be presumptuous to try to draw any firm conclusions about their relative importance as causal phenomena. Suffice it to say, however, that they all have a significant impact on the type of 'partnership' relationships which are successful in Japan.

Conclusion

This discussion of the main characteristics of Network Sourcing has shown that the system has many advantages over vertically integrated systems or the market driven system more typical in the West. These potential advantages are summarised in Table 8.7. The attempts by major Western multinationals to emulate Network Sourcing indicates that it is increasingly being recognised as an important source of competitive advantage. One major fear, however, is that its introduction in the West may result in 'cherry picking'. It may be, therefore, that, although many of the ten major characteristics of Network Sourcing have been adopted, it is in a piecemeal fashion and the full structure is rarely introduced. As a result only partial benefits may be achieved.

Table 8.7: Cross Regional Comparison of Automotive Suppliers

Average for Each Region	Japanese Japan	American America	All Europe
Supplier Performance:			
Die change times (minutes)	7.9	114.3	123.7
Lead time for new dies (weeks)	11.1	34.5	40.0
Machines per worker	7.4	2.5	2.7
Inventory levels (days)	1.5	8.1	16.3
No. of daily JIT deliveries	7.9	1.6	0.7
Parts defect (per car)	0.24	0.33	0.62
Supplier Involvement in Design:			
Engineering carried out by suppliers (% total hours)	51	14	35
Supplier propriety parts (%)	8	3	7
Black box parts (%)	62	16	39
Assembler design parts (%)	30	81	54
Supplier/Assembler Relations:			
Number of suppliers per assembly plant	170	509	442
Inventory level (days, for 8 parts)	0.2	2.9	2.0
Proportion of parts delivered just-in-time (%)	45.0	14.8	7.9
Proportion of parts single sourced (%)	12.1	69.3	32.9

Source: Adapted from: Womack et al (1990)

The characteristics of Network Sourcing that Western firms must valiantly seek to emulate are clearly supplier coordination and supplier development. The problem is that both of these activities require a significant input of time from the customer, and results are usually felt only in the medium to long term. There are major benefits for those who persevere and create a localised version of Network Sourcing. The case of Calsonic Llanelli Radiators provides a case study of a company which has been prepared to create supplier partnerships around a Supplier Association, the classic supplier coordination and development tool.

References

Blois, K.J. (1972) 'Vertical Quasi-Integration', *Journal of Industrial Economics,* 20, pp. 253-272.

Bruck, C. (1988) *Japanese Management of Subcontracting: The Dynamic Symbiosis,* MA Thesis, Keio University, Tokyo.

Carlisle, J.A. and Parker, R.C. (1989) *Beyond Negotiation: Redeeming Customer-Supplier Relationships,* Chichester, Wiley.

Christopher, M. (1992) *Logistics and Supply Chain Management: Strategies for Reducing Costs and Improving Services,* London, Pitman.

Dyer, J.H. (1994) 'Dedicated Assets: Japan's Manufacturing Edge,' *Harvard Business Review,* November-December, 72 (6), pp. 174-179.

Ellram, L.M. (1991) 'A Managerial Guideline for the Development and Implementation of Purchasing Partnerships', *International Journal of Purchasing and Materials Management,* 27 (3), pp. 2-8.

Farmer, D.H. and Ploos van Amstel, R. (1990) *Effective Pipeline Management: How To Manage Integrated Logistics,* Aldershot, Gower.

Ford, I.D (1980) 'The Development of Buyer-Supplier Relationships In Industrial Markets', *European Journal of Marketing,* 14 (5/6), pp. 339-353.

Giunipero, L. (1990) 'Motivating and Monitoring JIT Supplier Performance', *Journal of Purchasing and Materials Management*, 26 (3), Summer, pp. 19-24.

Hampson, R. (1992) 'Successful Supplier/Vehicle Manufacturer Relationships - Nissan's Experience in Europe', Boosting the Competitiveness of the Motor Industry Conference, IIR, The Waldorf, London, 30 November - 1 December.

Hines, P. (1994b) ' Network Sourcing: The Answer to the Single or Dual Sourcing Debate', *International Journal of Purchasing and Materials Management*, Tempe, Arizona, (forthcoming).

Hines, P. and Rich N. (1994) 'Focusing the Achievement of Continual Improvement Within the Supply Chain: An Automotive Case Study', *3rd International Conference of the International Purchasing & Supply Education & Research Association (IPSERA)*, Dyffryn House, University of Glamorgan, 28-30 March.

Ikeda, M. (1990) 'A Japanese Model for the Evolution of Subcontractors', *Kiezaigaku Ronsan (The Journal of Economics)*, 31 (5-6), November, pp. 91-104.

Ishikawa, K. (1985) *What is Total Quality Control? The Japanese Way*, Engelwood Cliffs, Prentice-Hall.

Kamath, R.R. and Liker, J.K. (1994) 'A Second Look at Japanese Product Development', *Harvard Business Review*, November-December, 72 (6), pp. 154-170.

Kinoshita H. (1986) 'The Role of Small Business', *Japan No. 376*, Japanese Embassy, London, 9 October.

Lamming, R. (1993) *Beyond Partnership: Strategies for Innovation and Lean Supply*, Hemel Hempstead, Prentice Hall.

Macbeth, D.K., Baxter, L.F., Ferguson, N. and Neil, G.C. (1989) 'Not Purchasing but Supply Chain Management', *Purchasing and Supply Management*, November, pp. 30-32.

Minato, T. (1991) 'The Development of Japanese Parts Supply Relationships: Past, Present and Future', *Customer-Supplier Relationship Study Tour*, EC-Japan Centre for Industrial Cooperation, 23 October, 1991.

Mitsui, I. (1991) 'A Unique Japanese Subcontracting System form a Global Point of View', *Customer-Supplier Relationships Study Tour*, EC-Japan Centre for Industrial Cooperation, Tokyo, 21 October, 1991.

Nishiguchi, T. (1987) 'Competing Systems of Automotive Components Supply: An Examination of the Japanese "Clustered Control" Model and the "Alps" Structure', *First Policy Forum IMVP*, May, pp 1-26.

Nishiguchi, T. (1989) Strategic Dualism: *An Alternative in Industrial Societies*, PhD Thesis, Nuffield College, Oxford University.

Nishiguchi, T. (1994) *Strategic Industrial Sourcing: The Japanese Advantage*, New York, Oxford University Press.

Norman, G. (1991) *Working In Partnership: Supplying the Japanese*, The Anglo-Japanese Economic Institute, London.

Sako, M. (1992) *Prices, Quality and Trust: Inter-Firm Relations in Britain & Japan*, Cambridge, Cambridge University Press.

Smith, C. (1982) 'Why Japan Still Thinks Small', *Financial Times*, London, 26 April.

Smitka, M. (1991) *Competitive Ties: Subcontracting in the Japanese Automotive Industry*, New York, Columbia University Press.

Womack, J.P., Jones, D.T. and Roos, D. (1990) *The Machine That Changed The World*, New York, Rawson.

CHAPTER 9

NETWORK SOURCING AT CALSONIC LLANELLI RADIATORS

Lyndon Jones

Introduction

Calsonic Llanelli Radiators was originally founded in Oxford in 1939. The Company moved to South Wales in 1943. The business was acquired by the Calsonic Corporation of Japan in 1989. Today, Calsonic Llanelli Radiators is part of the Calsonic International (Europe) Group of Companies which manufactures components for the European Automotive Industry. The products include catalytic converters, exhaust systems, climate control and cooling systems. This case study focuses on the practical application of network sourcing at Calsonic Llanelli Radiators to facilitate development, coordination and cooperation.

The automotive components industry is extremely competitive. To survive in this market place companies must continually strive to reduce costs, meet increasingly stringent quality standards, provide flexible and responsive logistics systems, compress the product development process and maintain a leading edge in manufacturing and product technology. It is not possible to meet these market challenges unless companies enlist the support of their supply network. The task is to unlock the competitive advantage that lies within the supply chain. To compete at world class levels requires a world class supply chain.

Section 1: The Supply Chain Challenge

- A significant proportion of current manufacturing costs are expended on Purchased Components/Raw Materials

- The Supply Network is a source of competitive advantage in terms of:

  - Cost
  - Quality
  - Logistics
  - New Product Development
  - Responsiveness/Flexibility

- To compete at World Class Levels requires a World Class Supply Network.

In response to these challenges Calsonic Llanelli Radiators embarked upon an External Resource Development Programme in 1988. A number of distinct phases can be identified within the programme.

Phase I   Building the Foundation
Period 1988 - 1991.
This phase concentrated on three fundamental issues:

- Quality Improvement
- Logistics Development
- Supply Base Reduction

The focus of the initial Quality Improvement Programme was on Suppliers Quality Systems and Process Controls. Training support was provided regarding techniques such as SPC & FMEA. The suppliers own QA initiatives towards reduction were actively facilitated and measured against targeted reduction of defect rates. When evidence existed that the suppliers processes were in control, the development concentration was switched to the Logistics Process.

Section 2: Logistics

- Increased Delivery Frequency/Timed Deliveries
- Delivery to Point of Use
- Guaranteed Delivery Quantities
- Guaranteed Quality (PPM)
- Bar Coding
- Electronic Trading Links

- Containerisation
- Use of Sequencing/Distribution Centres

Some of our existing suppliers were unable to meet the required Standards which contributed to the planned reduction in the total supply base.

Section 3: Supplier Base

Year		No. of Suppliers
1988	=	240
1990	=	178
1992	=	148
1994	=	105
1996	=	55 (target)

Phase II   Building the Framework of Existing and Future Relationships.
Period 1991 - 1993.

An important omission from Phase 1 was the creation of positive supplier relationships. Positive relationships can only be established in an operating environment of trust and integrity, supported by an open system of two way communication. This is a prerequisite to the establishment of any future meaningful collaboration. It was not possible to support this development activity with our total Supply Base. As a result it was necessary to focus on the strategically important segment of the supplier population. To facilitate the segmentation process a purchasing positioning model was developed.

It became apparent that the Strategic Sub Contractors category should become the focus of the relationship building programme. At this time we did not have the appropriate improvement mechanisms to facilitate this programme. Fortunately a relationship developed between the Welsh Development Agency and Peter Hines of the Cardiff Business School to consider Supplier Associations as being the appropriate development mechanism.

Section 4: Purchasing Positioning Model

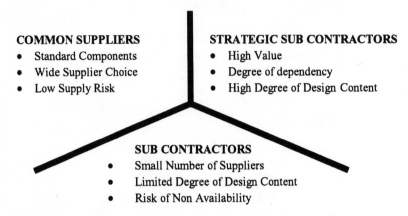

COMMON SUPPLIERS
- Standard Components
- Wide Supplier Choice
- Low Supply Risk

STRATEGIC SUB CONTRACTORS
- High Value
- Degree of dependency
- High Degree of Design Content

SUB CONTRACTORS
- Small Number of Suppliers
- Limited Degree of Design Content
- Risk of Non Availability

Section 5: Supplier Associations

Definition

A mutually benefiting group of the Company's strategic subcontractors brought together on a regular basis for the purpose of coordination, cooperation and development.

The company decided to pilot this approach and the first Association was formed in the Summer of 1991. Membership was restricted to strategic Sub-Contractors and their nominated First Tier Suppliers. The selection criteria and the Association membership is detailed in Section 6.

Section 6: Supplier Associations

Selection Criteria

- Degree of Dependency
- Degree of Unique/Joint Product Design
- Degree of Investment in People, Process and Products
- Positive Relationships

A second Association group was established six months later to include European Suppliers.

Section 7A:　Association Membership A

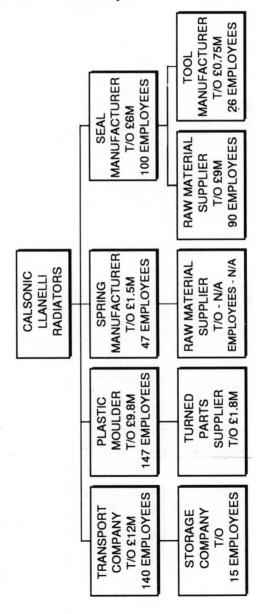

Section 7B: Association Membership B

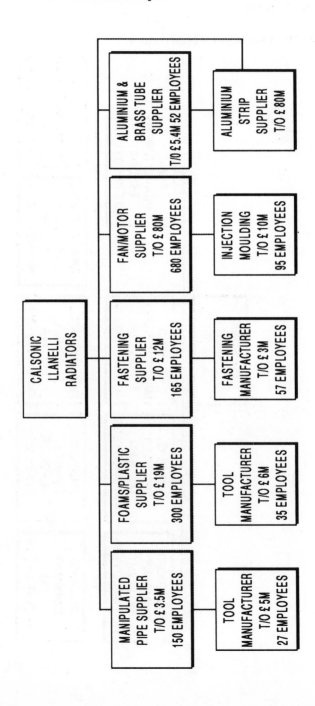

Subsequently these two groups were merged in 1992. The Aims and objectives of the Association are outlined below.

Section 8: Supplier Association

Aims and Objectives:

- Communication, coordination and deployment of Best Practice tools and techniques (Management and Manufacturing)
- Focus on joint weaknesses and inter company constraints
- Relationship decontamination

It was important to establish a datum point at the beginning of this process. A Benchmark Audit was developed in conjunction with Cardiff Business School. This audit covered soft and hard topics and formed the basis of a Strengths and Weakness evaluation.

The audit areas are outlined in Section 9.

Section 9: Benchmarking Audit

Areas Covered:

- Business Planning Processes and Implementation
- Quality Management and Process Control
- Operations Management
- Human Resource Management
- Kaizen Programmes
- Internal and External Relationship Audit Programmes
- Costing Systems

The Audit was used to set benchmarks against the Strategic Competitive Positioning Model again developed by the Cardiff Business School.

Section 10: Competitive Positioning Model

Stages of Development

- Stage I   -   Price Competition
- Stage II   -   Quality Competition
- Stage III   -   Close Cooperation (Supplier Development)
- Stage IV   -   Strategic Partnership (Lean Supply)
- Stage V   -   World Class Competitor

The summary data was utilised to target joint weakness for best practice workshop.

Section 11: Best Practice Workshops

- Time to Market
- Kaizen and 3 Day Kaizen
- EDI/Bar Coding
- Value Engineering/Value Analysis
- Benchmarking
- Business Planning
- Customer Initiatives
  - Rover RG 2000 DE/JIT
  - Nissan NX 96

The Association Membership also determined a programme of continuous improvement for all member Companies in the key processes of quality, cost, delivery, design and management ability.

Section 12: Joint Objectives

Medium Term Deliverables

- **T.Q.M.**
  - Extension of TQM Culture to Suppliers
  - Focus on Kaizen Improvements
  - Training in Kaizen Group Activities
  - On Site Facilitation of Kaizen Groups

- **Target Costs**
  - ◆ Develop Understanding Amongst Suppliers
  - ◆ Discussion of Methods
  - ◆ Application of Open Book Accounting
  - ◆ Utilisation of **'Three Day'** Kaizen Event

- **Logistics**
  - ◆ Increased Delivery Frequency and Timed Deliveries
  - ◆ Delivery to Point of Use
  - ◆ Guaranteed Delivery Quantities
  - ◆ Guaranteed Delivery Quality (PPM Levels)
  - ◆ Bar Coding
  - ◆ E.D.I. Trading Links
  - ◆ Containerisation
  - ◆ Sequence/D.C.Centres

- **Product Development**
  - ◆ Faster Time to Market
  - ◆ Increased Design Role for Suppliers
  - ◆ Earlier Involvement in Design Process

These joint improvement activities assisted the relationship decontamination process by:

- Cross Company visits
- Joint sharing of operations problems
- Shared learning programmes
- Shared benchmarking information
- Guest personnel

Phase III   Developments of Strategic Relationships
Lean Supply
Period 1994 Onwards

A programme assessment took place early in 1994 to measure the degree of change in relationship and operational integrity in the key areas of quality, cost, logistics, product development and management capability. The results of the assessment were positive, therefore, it was decided to accelerate the improvement programme to encompass Lean Supply. The catalyst or engine room for improvement would continue to be the Supplier Association. It was decided to map the attributes of a lean supply chain from a process and an organisational prospective.

Section 13: Lean Supply Attributes

- Absolute minimum inventory
- Elimination of defective parts
- Elimination of machine breakdowns PPM/TPM
- High degree of flexibility and responsiveness
- Short order to delivery lead times
- Build only to customers' orders

Lean Organisation Attributes

- Flat Structures
- Employee Empowerment/Teamwork
- Single Status Employment Conditions
- Continuous Improvement Culture
- Emphasis on Innovation
- People Development
- Project Management (Cross Functional Teams)
- Seamless Enterprises (Cross Functional Management)

Each attribute is expressed as a series of measurable elements. These elements are charted on a radar diagram with a Lean Supply benchmark residing on the outer perimeter. An Audit programme is currently in progress to map each Association member's performance against the lean supply metrics. This will provide the new datum point for future improvements.

LEAN SUPPLY METRICS

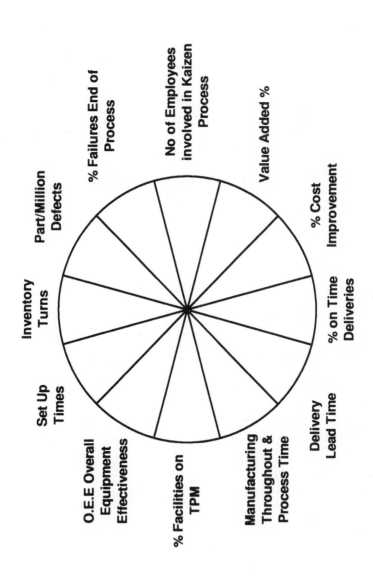

190

PART E:

EDI AND PURCHASING

CHAPTER 10

PROCESS TECHNOLOGY, EDI AND REGULATORY RULES: THE IMPLICATIONS FOR PURCHASING OF ESIS

Andrew Cox and David Court

Introduction

There can be little doubt that technology is one of the main drivers of change in markets. Whether we consider the impact of cotton spinning machines and the early industrial factory system (Landes, 1972), or more recent developments like motor car and Fordist principles of industrial organisation (Womack, 1990), it is clear that technology is one of the most important factors affecting value and supply chains.

Technology has a significant impact because it increases the rate of efficiency and productivity of labour inputs to the production of goods and services; if this were not so, no company would invest its capital in the process of replacing labour with machinery.

While there are obviously heavy initial costs in the purchase and siting of machinery, firms are only prepared to do this if they believe that the long-term benefits outweigh the short-term costs. The short-term cost for firms is heavy initial capital expenditure; the short-term cost for society is unemployment as displaced workers lose their jobs. The history of industrial development demonstrates, however, that after an initial displacement of unskilled and semi-skilled workers, more, rather than less, jobs have eventually been created (Landes, 1972).

Since the second world war the pace of technology change has progressed rapidly. Many of these innovations: the radar, the computer, the jet engine, nuclear fusion and rocket and space technology, were, in fact, a direct consequence of research and development programmes

stimulated by the requirements of the war. Whatever one may think about
the morality of this there is little doubt that the impact of war proves the
general dictum that *'necessity is the mother of invention'*.

Innovation does not, however, result solely from the impact of war. In
industrial markets, whether for goods or services, the relationship between
regulatory structures and competition are also key variables which
determine innovation and the need for new technology. While this chapter
cannot deal with these issues in detail it is possible to outline some of the
major factors which shape innovation within markets and their impact on
supply chain management.

We discuss some of these factors below, and then show how
technological innovation in information technology, related specifically to
electronic data interchange (EDI) and multi-media, may have a profound
impact on purchasing and supply relationships in the future. We conclude
this chapter with an indication of how these changes may affect public
sector purchasing. This is achieved through a brief overview of a new
purchasing system which has been recently introduced by the public sector
in Northern Ireland. The potential beneficial impact of EDI on private
sector purchasing is discussed in the final chapter in the book through a
case study of an EDI-Kanban system at Avery Berkel.

Regulation, Markets and Technological Innovation

Why do private companies and public organisations need new technology?
There may be many subjective reasons - associated with status, power,
ignorance and, even corruption - why people *want* new technology; this
does not tell us however, why they objectively *need* it. In this section we
will discuss some of the reasons why the private sector and the public sector
need rather than *want* new technology.

In the **private sector,** where firms must compete for survival, the need
for new technology is essential because only those firms which can produce
goods and services efficiently, and with high quality at low prices, will
satisfy and retain their customers. Obviously firms can discover and patent
new products and processes which give them a lead in the market, and this
is a primary reason why technology is important.

New technology, which provides innovative products and services,
cannot, however, be kept a secret. It can be patented but it cannot be
insulated forever from normal market pressures. This means that as soon
as a new technology, which creates a new product or service, is discovered

and becomes known in the market then, sooner or later, there will be a search by competitors for cheaper methods of production. There will also be continuous pressure for the development of additional innovative applications of the new technology.

We can see the process at work with the development of micro-chip technology. After the second world war IBM was able to dominate world markets for computer products and services, especially in corporate data processing markets. The reasons for this were clearly associated with technological leadership and the costs of entry for competitors in the market place. This domination started to unravel in the 1970s and 1980s due to technological innovation in the form of the micro-chip. This technological innovation allowed the production of smaller and smaller computers with incredible memories and functional capabilities.

The development of the chip gave rise to new products, like the personal computer (PC), which are now available at a price which is affordable by individuals as well as by firms. In this instance the technology, by reducing the costs of production and by maintaining functional capability and quality, massively expanded the potential market for computers, and also destroyed IBM's dominance of the market for corporate data processing.

The problem did not end here for IBM. The development of the micro-chip may have destroyed IBM's traditional market for very expensive and physically cumbersome corporate computer systems, but it also left them poorly placed to compete in the fast growing personal computer market. Increasingly, new entrepreneurs and companies were able to enter the market and to source their production in cheap labour markets in the Pacific Rim and Asia. One of the major reasons for this was the fact that IBM was no longer able to link the purchase of the hardware to the use of IBM software.

The real problem for IBM was not just that it had locked itself into old technology, and missed the market potential of innovative technology, it had also misunderstood that the real growth in the market would also be for software applications and not just for the hardware systems which they had heavily invested in. The rise of Bill Gates' Microsoft is ample testimony to IBM's short-sighted and complacent approach to technological innovation.

The message from the computer industry is therefore axiomatic. New technology destroys the old market relationships and, in doing so, creates new market opportunities for existing goods and services. It also creates potentially new products and services which have been used before. What this means in practice is that when new technology enters markets it radically restructures existing supply and sourcing relationships.

In the case of computers the new technology caused the basic sourcing and supply relationships in the market to physically relocate away from North America to the Pacific Rim. The basic reason for this was due to the impact which the new technology had on the computer value chain. Historically, because IBM was able to dominate the supply of the technology and the software for corporate customers, IBM controlled the value chain. The price of the end product was largely determined by what IBM decided. This meant that the question of where the product was supplied from was of little significance and, in practice, IBM sourced primarily from local suppliers.

The new technology destroyed IBM's dominance of the corporate market and also created a new market for PCs and for user friendly software and games. IBM was not able to control this market and, because the costs of entry had drastically fallen due to the new technology, it was possible for relatively small and innovative companies to enter the market. Since the costs of entry were relatively low, and there is a huge effective demand for the new products and services, it was inevitable that there would be a rapacious competition amongst entrants to claim market share.

The relatively free market has therefore witnessed the classic symptoms of open competition: too many market entrants, low margins and fierce competition for market share. The consequences of this has been, of course, a search by firms for low cost and high quality suppliers around the world in an attempt to find a competitive edge. The value chain is no longer controlled by one major player and firms have, as a result, to find the lowest cost and highest quality sources of supply if they are to stay in the market. The luxury of sourcing locally, irrespective of cost, quality or value, is no longer available in this market.

One has to be careful, however, about assuming that this is so in all markets at all times. Clearly, the maturity of markets and their degree of openness will depend on the age of the technology, the relative costs of entry for new participants and the size of the existing players. There is, however, a further factor which crucially affects the openness of markets and, therefore, the impact of new technology within them. This factor is the regulatory regime within which firms operate.

The regulatory regime means those laws, policies and rules by which legitimate and authoritative institutions maintain order and stability within a given territorial area. In common language we are referring here to the rules by which nation-states govern a territorial area over which the indigenous populace recognise their legitimate right to do so. These rights to make binding and authoritative decisions, are normally also backed by the threat of coercive violence. The state also commands a monopoly of the use of these instruments of violence within a given territorial area (Weber 1968, Cox et al, 1985).

Since the population of a given territorial area acquiesces to and/or supports the rule of law from given state institutions, private firms are always operating in tension. This tension arises because firms idealistically espouse the benefits of free markets but also fear the consequences of them. On the one hand, therefore, some firms want markets to be open and unregulated by public bodies - especially if they have state of the art technology and low cost, high quality products. On the other hand, some firms want markets to be regulated by public bodies in order to protect their market share against more efficient competitors and suppliers. This tension also exists within the citizenry of any nation-state: some workers are sanguine about the employment consequences of competition, other workers are not.

The tension between technological leaders and technological laggards is endemic to capitalist economies and a major cause of nation-state policy-making over trade and commercial issues. Nation-states cannot ignore the imperatives of the market, but they must also respond to the demands of their own citizens for a decent standard of living and employment security. Markets do not and cannot, therefore, operate in isolation. The way in which technology affects any national market for a given product and service will, therefore, depend not just on the competitors within that national market, but also upon the way in which national policy-makers regulate that market.

The regulatory structure, whether markets for particular goods or services are open or closed, is therefore a key determinant of the scope for, and pace of, technological change within national markets. There are also regional (EC, NAFTA) and international (GATT) regulatory regimes which shape market openness (Cox and Greenwold 1993, Cox and Sanderson 1994a & 1994b). What is perhaps less appreciated, however, is that changes in these regulatory regimes which remove or impose artificial barriers to trade, like tariffs or preferential national purchasing rules (Cox 1993), will have a profound impact on purchasing and supply relationships.

While recent research demonstrates that there has been little observable impact on the national location of sourcing and supply for public sector contracts in the EU as a result of the ending of artificial barriers to trade by the Single Market initiative, there may well be significant sourcing and supply changes taking place beneath the surface (Cox 1993, Cox and Furlong, 1994a, 1994b, 1994c).

The reason for this removal of national preferential purchasing rules may not have led to any significant increase in the numbers of contracts being won by non-nationally based suppliers to the public sector, but it may well have led to a significant increase in cross-border sourcing and supply from those local firms still winning national contracts. This arises because deregulation forces firms to become more proactive in their sourcing and supply, due to the anticipated pressure from potential new market entrants.

What all of this means is that regulatory rules have a symbiotic relationship with the scope for, and pace of, technological innovation and, therefore, the level of competition in markets. The degree to which the development of micro-chip technology will, therefore, affect any national market is dependent, in the short-term, on the regulatory structure which restrains or welcomes this innovation. Eventually, however, it appears to be the case that regulatory rules cannot do more than temporarily halt these new innovations. In the long-term new technology gradually enters markets legally (or illegally) as companies find ways to circumvent regulatory rules.

The conclusion that one has to draw from this discussion is that private firms *need* new technology to survive in the long-term. They need it for two reasons: they must innovate and find new products and services to create new markets; and they must use new technology to reduce the costs and add value to the processes by which they create existing goods and services in the market. The reasons why the public sector *needs* new technology are not really very dissimilar.

Unless the **public sector** is directly involved in the production of goods and services in the form of nationalised industries there is no commercial or competitive rationale for the adoption of new technology. Nevertheless, new technology is essential to the delivery of many of the services for which the public sector is normally responsible. It does not matter whether we are discussing health, education or employment services, most public goods involve the purchase of physical goods and services. While labour costs are a significant and, in many cases, the major element in public service provision, the purchase of goods and services from outside the provider bureaucracy is still a significant element of total public expenditure. This means that the public sector also has the same vested interest in technological innovation as the private sector; because lower cost and higher value products and services are crucial to the delivery of a better level and quality of public service.

Technological innovation is also crucial in the provision of many public services because it also provides the opportunity for innovative treatments and processes. New technology in healthcare has meant that heart disease need not cause premature death, and hip replacements are now common among geriatric patients. New technology, especially EDI and computer based technology, can also assist in the delivery of information so that speedier and more effective decisions can be made, and with the requisite information available for comprehensive analysis of any particular problem. For all of these reasons the public sector needs technological innovation in much the same way as the private sector. Despite this, as we discuss below, the application of new technology is both an opportunity and a challenge for the private and public sectors.

The Challenge and Opportunity of Innovation:
The Case of EDI, Multi-Media and Information Technology

The major challenge which technological innovation poses for both the public and private sectors is that, while it is clearly in their interests to adopt it, such innovation must be implemented against the barriers of standard operating procedures (SOPs) within organisations. This problem is particularly true when it comes to the introduction of EDI related information technology. The major opportunity for both sectors is that EDI technology offers the possibility of substantially reducing transaction costs in the process of purchasing goods and services for an organisation. We address the challenges and opportunities facing the implementation of EDI systems in general in this section, before looking at what may be possible in the public sector in the future. The opportunities for transforming private sector sourcing and supply are described in chapter 11.

The adoption of new technology in the form of EDI and multi-media systems provides the opportunity for purchasing professionals to reduce transaction costs within the organisation. All too often 80% of purchasing staff time is spent in order processing and expediting tasks. These clerical functions are associated with paper based systems, in which the task has low potential for value added but, at the same time, consumes tremendous amounts of staff time. By finding ways to eliminate these clerical and non-value adding tasks public and private organisations can reduce transaction costs and provide the space for purchasing professionals to develop their strategic value to the organisation.

A simple example will provide clear evidence of what can be achieved. When cars roll off the production line the company knows how many specific components it takes to produce one car. It follows, therefore, that the company can dispense with complex and heavily bureaucratic order and stock holding systems if it, first, chooses preferred suppliers capable of providing just-in-time sourcing and, second, pay them, without orders and invoices, on the basis of the number of components per car produced monthly. This simple example of strategic thinking, currently operated by Nissan, massively reduces transaction costs.

The problem is, of course, that there is tremendous opposition to this type of order processing system which reduces transaction interfaces, because there is a fear that it will result in massive job losses and because it challenges other SOPs within the organisation. Financial and accounting systems are nearly always set up in such a way to increase rather than reduce transaction costs. Overcoming these obstacles within the organisation can be extremely difficult but, as argued in chapter 1, it is essential that these internal battles be won if a professional approach to external resource management is to be achieved.

The advent of EDI systems means that purchasing based on traditional SOPs can be radically transformed through the use of technological innovation. The major benefit that can be achieved is through a reduction in transaction costs as a result of increases in the speed of the purchasing process. The impact of this new technology will be far-reaching and, potentially, global in its impact. With existing technology it is now possible for instant, up-to-date information about the price and availability of goods and services to be available to purchasers twenty four hours a day. This offers purchasers closer and more efficient links with their suppliers, and reinforces the development of just-in-time and partnership sourcing relationships.

The benefits of EDI multi-media systems can be defined therefore as follows:

a) Supplier Advantage

The availability of such services at low cost to all businesses, particularly small and medium sized enterprises, enables them to compete more effectively across wide global markets. The system removes the major difficulties associated with communicating information to and from remote locations by the more traditional approaches of cold calling with printed catalogues and telephone selling.

b) Purchasing Advantage

Traditionally printed information is an increasing problem for any large purchasing organisation, as not only is it bulky and rapidly out of date, but it is difficult to integrate into modern systems and expensive to communicate. Current information on specification, price and availability is essential but printed paper cannot provide this information efficiently to purchasers in a rapidly changing market place.

An illustration of the practical problem occurs when a Purchasing Manager visits any large trade exhibition. Purchasers would find it impossible to collect just one copy of each piece of printed information available. Bulk is not the only problem. It is difficult to know if any catalogue in any Purchasing Office is up to date. How can anyone be certain that the specifications or prices have not changed? A common practice is to send out for price and specification amendments for catalogue holders to be up to date. In practice a very large percentage of respondents either do not bother to provide the information or only include some of the required amendments. These are real practical problems for any purchasing organisation.

The traditional purchasing model is to follow a route which includes looking for a catalogue, checking if the information is correct, writing out a requisition, sending it off to be authorised and, then, forwarding it to the Buying Department. This is hardly an efficient, customer friendly purchasing process which aids lean supply. It is clearly not appropriate for purchasers to subject customers to a time consuming bureaucratic process that can take 5 to 10 days before an order is placed. Purchasing in the past tried to develop by improving supplier performance through, for example, 'just in time' techniques. It has also introduced computerised stock control systems, but little attention has been given to the total purchasing and supply process which starts with the requisitioner or end user. Now, with the EDI systems it is possible for purchasing to become the agent of their customers. Taking a strategic view purchasing is, at best, a service providing function which must provide a fast efficient service to ultimate customers within the organisation. EDI systems clearly provide a vehicle for achieving this in the future.

Currently many purchasing systems, particularly in large bureaucratic organisations, are an inefficient mixture of manual and electronic processes. These dualistic systems are necessary to complete the purchasing cycle. In the USA, in September 1993 the report of the National Performance Review entitled *From Red Tape to Results -*

Creating a Government that Works Better and Costs Less (Gore, 1993) these problems were discussed in some detail, under four key headings:

1) Cutting Red Tape

2) Putting the Customer First

3) Empowering Employees to Get Results

4) Cutting Back to Basics.

   In this report the largest expenditure savings were expected to come from the streamlining of bureaucracy. The section on public sector procurement clearly identified the need to assist in this process by encouraging more procurement innovation. This was to be achieved by establishing simplified acquisition procedures, lowering costs and reducing bureaucracy, as well as by encouraging best value procurement. The major goal here was to achieve substantial savings by reducing the size, complexity and paper-inertia within the purchasing bureaucracy, rather than relying, primarily, on pressuring suppliers to cut prices in the traditional adversarial way.

   One way to do this is through facilitating end users to use EDI systems both to order goods directly from suppliers and to communicate directly with other managers in the organisation. Professional purchasers are, thereby, freed to concentrate on implementing and managing strategic purchasing strategy. Obviously this may result in a reduction of the absolute number of low grade, clerical purchasing staff within an organisation, but it will free purchasing specialists to concentrate on "adding value not cost". This would be achieved by concentrating on facilitating framework agreements and organising the 'call-off' contracts for end-users to utilise. To achieve this, however, SOPs within organisations must be addressed first. If they can be, then significant reductions in transaction costs are possible. An example of what is possible is outlined in the next section.

The European Satellite Information Services (ESIS) in Northern Ireland

Northern Ireland is not always associated with high technology yet it has one of the most advanced telecommunication systems in Europe. This system provides a direct access, fibre-optic network throughout the province which is significantly more powerful than anything that exists elsewhere in Europe. Such networks, with the power to instantly communicate data and images, are basic requirements for multi-media systems in the future. This new technology will revolutionise the way business is undertaken in the future and purchasing will be no exception.

ESIS in Northern Ireland is a key example of this new form of trading. It is a massive open system catalogue library, constantly updated for users, with no need for expensive manual intervention at user level. The system can be left switched on and the information provided on it is automatically updated. In this way ESIS provides suppliers with the ability to maintain their product information either on an interactive basis or via batch product updates. Suppliers register with ESIS which acts as an independent confidential data library. Consumer organisations are able to contract with their own suppliers to take the service. The suppliers can then notify ESIS of the data transmission requirements for their individual customers and consumer organisations. The economies of scale which are thereby produced are available to the consumer and supplier alike.

By providing accurate product data in this way the efficiency of the whole ordering chain from internal requisition through to delivery and payment is increased. Suppliers obtain a significant advantage in that their products are accurately presented to clients in a timely fashion. This adds a new dimension to selling and enhances a firm's ability to promote its products. Customers also have added confidence in the knowledge that the goods they order, and at the price quoted, are what they will ultimately receive.

The system works in the following manner. Suppliers provide their latest catalogue requirements to the ESIS Centre with product specifications, descriptions and prices. The data may also include their logo, branding and even pictures of the products, if required. The resulting database is formatted into a definitive up-to-date electronic library of products which is then made available to consumers by direct satellite broadcast, using a common transmission standard. The signal is then received on low cost (domestic type) satellite receivers and fed into a PC or local network server, where it automatically maintains a current data base of products and services. Use of the service is made easy for the customer. Powerful plain language search and display facilities enable fast and accurate tracing of the products required. There is no need to enter descriptions, prices or product codes, the selected items are automatically extracted to enable fast production of electronic requisitions or orders.

With ESIS, most time-consuming tasks disappear. The key gains are that one does not have to

- hunt for the right catalogue and the exact items.

- check if the prices and specifications are up-to-date

- manually copy the details for input to one's own system.

The familiar paperchase gives way to an efficient, fast, user-friendly process which allows the buyer to concentrate on adding value, not perpetuating slow, costly, paper-based systems.

Conclusions

While there will be no completely paperless trading in the short term, in the medium term there may well be. In the interim, however, there is a massive opportunity for purchasers to cut down paper mountains and, in so doing, enhance the efficiency of purchasing organisations.

Eventually all professional purchasing organisations, if they are interested in lean supply, will need a comprehensive electronic trading strategy. It is possible that this will be more than a simple 'add on' EDI package to existing computerised stores systems. EDI is machine-to-machine direct communication, and it is therefore inevitable that it will be necessary to 'staff the system' not 'systemise the existing staffing'. The point is that processes will fundamentally have to change as a result of the new technology. Multi-media and EDI may well provide the most significant change in the distribution of commercial information since the invention of printing. If this comes about it will be because technological innovation has reduced transaction costs and assisted in the process of adding value and reducing costs. An alternative use for EDI, which assists in the development of private sector supply, is discussed in the next chapter.

Bibliography

Cox, A. (1993) *Public Procurement in the EC. Volume 1: Single Market Rules and the Enforcement Regime After 1992*, Boston, Earlsgate Press.

Cox, A. and Furlong, P. (1994a) *Cross Border Trade and Cross Border Contract Awards: The Dilemma at the Heart of the EU Procurement Rules*, CPRU Working Paper, No.1, CPRU, University of Birmingham.

Cox, A. and Furlong, P. (1994b) *The Jury is Still Out: Contract Awards Under the EU Utilities Procurement Rules*, CPRU Working Paper, No. 2, CPRU, University of Birmingham.

Cox, A. and Furlong, P. (1994c) *EU Public Works Contracts and the Nationality of Supply*, CPRU Working Paper, No. 3, CPRU, University of Birmingham.

Cox, A., Furlong, P. and Page, E. (1985) *Power in Capitalist Society: Theories Cases and Methods*, Brighton, Harvester Press.

Cox, A. and Greenwold, S. (1993) 'The Legal and Structural Obstacles to Free trade in the US Procurement Market', *Public Procurement Law Review*, Number 5, pp. 237-252.

Cox, A. and Sanderson, J. (1994a) 'From the Mobilisation of Bias to trade Wars: The Making and Implementing of the EC Utilities procurement Rules', *European Journal of Public Policy*, 1 (2), Autumn, pp. 263-282.

Cox, A. and Sanderson, J. (1994b) *The Political Economy of Bilateral Managed Trade: Explaining the US-EU Conflict Over Market Entry Rules for Utilities Procurement Contracts*, CPRU Working Paper, No. 4, CPRU, University of Birmingham.

Landes, D. (1972) *The Unbound Prometheus*, Cambridge, Cambridge University Press.

Weber, M. (1968) *Economy and Society*, Berkley, University of California Press.

Womack, J.P. et al, (1990) *The Machine That Changed the World*, New York, Rawson Association.

CHAPTER 11

AN EDI - KANBAN REPLENISHMENT SYSTEM AT AVERY BERKEL

Neil Roberts, Gareth Arnold and David Small

Summary

The use of Electronic Data Interchange (EDI) as a method of transmitting commercial information has become widespread in the last decade. In most cases this has simply meant converting existing paper documents into computer messages. Recently, techniques have been developed that incorporate EDI with advanced replenishment techniques e.g. Kanban. The benefits of such EDI systems are not always readily visible to business areas other than the immediate user community. This article outlines the approach taken at Avery Berkel and, hopefully, illustrates the real benefits to be gained from this approach and also some of the most common problems encountered.

At Avery Berkel, EDI has not been implemented in isolation, nor imposed upon existing working practices, but as part of a programme of strategic development. Joint Purchasing, Material Control and Production strategies have been developed, by seeking consensus from all interested parties, and then implemented over an 18-24 month period. The EDI system was initially implemented into a Surface Mount Technology (SMT) production cell and has been 'live' for approximately 14 months; this chapter focuses only on this area. The benefits revealed are:

- Increasing stock turns nearly threefold (and still rising)
- Inventory reduction (£440K to £220K)
- Elimination of production shortages
- Improved internal and external communications
- Improved relationships with key suppliers

- Reducing non value adding activities such as scheduling, kitting and expediting
- Reduction in unit prices of components

The return on investment has been approximately 90 times in the first year. We have only just begun but can see a path to wider usage of EDI not only as a replenishment vehicle, but also to exploit the benefits in other areas of our business, particularly administration functions.

Company Background and Organisation

Avery Berkel is one of the world's largest producers of weighing equipment and food processing equipment with factories in Birmingham, Rotterdam, USA and India. Worldwide sales exceed £200 million per annum with over 4,000 employees worldwide. Owned by GEC plc the group was formed when Berkel was acquired by GEC Avery Ltd.

The UK Weighing Products division employs around 750 people and ships £31 million per annum of manufactured products. These vary from electronic retail and scientific scales to heavy industrial platforms. The company commands a large market share in the UK.

Manufacturing was reorganised in 1992 into self-contained production cells. Each cell manager has a staff of assembly, quality, production and material control personnel and is wholly responsible for the output, quality and costs associated with his cell.

Purchasing is organised as a central strategic function responsible for sourcing, cost reduction, contract negotiation and supplier development. The day to day material control activities, scheduling, kitting and expediting, are performed within each production cell.

December 1992 - The Problems being Faced

At the outset of the project, December 1992, there were many problems in a number of functional areas that required attention.

Material Control

Material Requirement Planning (MRP) was running on a monthly basis but the administration cycle was approximately 6 weeks. The material controllers treated every part in the same way regardless of value or product type. Thus 'A' Class items were treated exactly the same as 'C' class. There were frequent production programme changes resulting in many production shortages. Delivery of all production materials was scheduled for the beginning of each manufacturing period. Scheduled quantities were 'massaged' for safety reasons.

Purchasing

A very large production supply base existed supporting a fairly low annual spend. Each part was sourced from what was considered to be the cheapest supplier. There was a tendency to work directly with component manufacturers as distribution was considered too expensive. Service was not really a purchasing consideration. Purchasing was being treated as an administration function with buyers as order placers, and with components, manufacturers and types specified by engineers.

Assembly

Early in 1993, the company was struggling with an external SMT board sub-contractor whose requirements for large batch manufacturing were at odds with our need to have small batch sizes. Avery Berkel therefore decided to invest £750,000 to bring SMT board production in-house.

The prime requirement was to create a SMT production cell that was flexible in its response to customer demand by producing the smallest batch possible. This cell would be set up to run alongside the existing, conventional PCB production cell.

The working practices in use across the conventional PCB cell could not meet the requirements of the new SMT cell. Therefore new ways of working had to be devised for assembly, quality, production and material control processes.

Overview of EDI

What is EDI?

The National Computing Centre (NCC) defines Electronic Data Interchange (EDI) as "The transfer of structured data, by agreed message standards from one computer system to another, by electronic means".

Both the automotive industry and the food retail industry have been active in the development of computer to computer generation of purchase orders over the last ten years. Both have interests in retaining only small amounts of stock of items and controlling inventory in order to be able to react quickly to the demands placed on the company. This would prove costly and difficult without some fast means of communicating current and ever changing requirements. Formats of communication have evolved in order that EDI capable companies are now able to reduce their costs without increasing those of their suppliers (and therefore the costs of the goods).

A number of message standards, communications protocols and operating methods are used in different fields of worldwide business. We shall confine our interest to the EDIFACT standard. Electronic Data Interchange For Administration, Commerce and Transport, (EDIFACT) is the EC and UN sponsored set of message standards intended to cover all areas of trade and provide messages flexible enough to cater for all needs, but rigid enough to be interpreted by all systems that need to use it without adjustment. The standard now has ISO number 9735. It is a result of the attempt to reconcile message standards derived from the United Nations Trade Data Interchange (UNTDI) standard, on which many European messages are based, and the American National Standards Institute (ANSI) X.12 standard, which is widely used in North America and between US companies and their subsidiaries. The use of EDIFACT as a message standard is growing rapidly, most companies taking up EDI for the first time now choose EDIFACT for their messages and in some business communities it is planned to change to EDIFACT and to abandon lesser used current standards.

Why EDI?

Most businesses handle huge amounts of paper documents for a variety of purposes. A large number of these are simply to support the procurement of, and payment for, goods and services that the company needs in order to produce its own goods and services, and they thereby generate more paperwork. A survey carried out in 1984 by AT&T Istel and the Institute of Physical Distribution found that there were some 3.2 billion documents involved in the order/invoice cycle in the UK annually, and that the average processing cost of each document was £10.00 to give a gross cost of £32 billion. This of course will have grown in the ten years since. Having sent and received these millions of documents, much time and effort is then spent correcting errors that are contained within the data, very often as a result of a mis-key from some point when the information was entered into a computer system.

EDI cuts through the non-value adding, bureaucratic processes that feed on this mountain of paper, both to generate it and to handle it once produced. EDI helps to automate the office and reduce the costs of administration, allowing the expensive machines that were purchased to keep control, to talk to each other without clumsy, error prone, human interpreters. EDI will allow many processes to be simplified, improving the speed of response of the entire business. But EDI is just the technology that enables these improvements to take place, by providing timely and accurate information and by taking advantage of improvements in telecommunications and greater reliability of business computers. The effects of this combination upon logistics are profound because it increases the proportion of value added activities to non-value adding activities.

The principal interest in EDI for Avery Berkel was the transmission of Purchase Orders which could contain details of the sender and the addressee, plus line items with delivery schedule details and payment terms.

Strategy Development and Implementation

The three main strategies to develop and implement these were Purchasing, Material Control and the SMT cell setup. Each of these will now be discussed in more detail.

Purchasing

In November 1992 the Purchasing department had an annual spend of approximately £15 million and a supply base of 350 production suppliers. With no clear strategy in place the key problems could be seen as:

- Too many vendors to support, giving poor economies
- Buying each item from cheapest source, with the added large administrative overhead associated
- Buyers were considered to be 'Order Placers', performing low value activities
- Because of the large vendor count we were unable to develop strong relationships with preferred suppliers
- Engineers were specifying suppliers, not components

The first key strategy was to develop a supplier development programme. The key elements to this programme were:

- Supplier Reduction
- Purchase Agreements with targeted Suppliers
- Simplified Logistics Cycle with targeted Suppliers (in line with the material control strategy)

The key driver was to get the Purchasing team to add value to the process and to reduce the non-value tasks to a minimum.

Supplier Reduction

The task here was quite simple and by analysing where our money was spent we could easily identify the number of suppliers really needed to support our production processes. The hardest task was to select the 'right' suppliers that would meet our needs in all areas. The graph in Figure 11.1 illustrates how our spend was distributed at the initiation of our reduction programme and how it has been affected by it.

Figure 11.1:

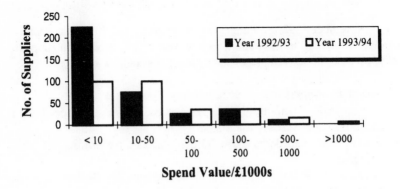

Spend Distribution - FY92/93 & FY93/94

The graph clearly shows a skew at the wrong end of the distribution. There were too many suppliers with too little value. The Purchasing team identified a medium-term (2 year) reduction target to 180. This was to be achieved by resourcing the current supply base and without additional engineering resource to achieve it. Each Buyer then drew up their own reduction plan and set about implementing it. Eventually a long-term target of 150 was established, but the team felt this could only be achieved with the input of additional engineering resource. As a result of this activity the supplier base has reduced from 340 to 207 production suppliers. The target for the end of the current financial year is 180.

The graph in Figure 11.2 below illustrates the achievement of the reduction plan.

Figure 11.2:

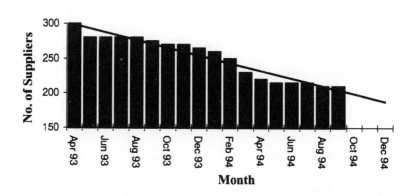

Another major question to be addressed was whether to buy from Distribution Channels or direct from manufacturers. Traditionally Avery Berkel had dealt directly with manufacturers of components, however it is now felt that we can achieve better value for money by looking closely at the choice of component suppliers and distributors.

Choice of Electronic Component Suppliers

Having identified the suppliers who could best meet our short- and long-term requirements, an electronic tender document (1500 items worth £2 million per annum) was sent out to six targeted component distributors and analysed on return with regard to the parts base covered and total cost of the supply package. In this way 60 suppliers were ultimately reduced to 20 with an identified further potential for reduction to six. As a general rule it is now a requirement of any new supplier to be or become EDI capable. The results of the exercise have been quite startling:

- Reduction in supply base of 30 suppliers
- Annual savings of £200K

This was achieved in a climate of great uncertainty in the electronic components market when many products were on allocation and prices were rising. The benefits for Avery Berkel in moving to distribution were, and still are, manifold:

- Potential of EDI Kanban,
- Service the short lead times necessary to meet changing customer demand,
- Lower cost of individual components as a total package,
- Sourcing a larger number of components from fewer sources, and
- Savings in our administration costs (e.g. scheduling time, goods receiving time, carrier costs, and ordering costs)

Purchase Agreements/Better Relationships with targeted Suppliers

Another key desire was to create much stronger relationships with a number of suppliers who are seen as being strategically important to Avery Berkel. These suppliers were principally identified by spend and by the type of technology being supplied. By using the reduction process we were able to give our targeted suppliers a much larger slice of the available spend. Obviously this has benefits for both parties. The type of agreement developed, and still developing, is one which moves away from formal legal documents to a description of what each company is prepared to give to the relationship. Each agreement is tailored to the needs of that specific relationship.

The principle of each agreement is the commitment that we as the buyer make, as well as what the supplier gives in return. The desire is to have a relationship where joint discussion takes place, rather than punitive legal action.

The graph figure 11.3 below shows progress against our plan to have our top 50 suppliers (by value or technology importance) on agreement by the end of the current financial year.

Figure 11.3:

Purchase Agreements

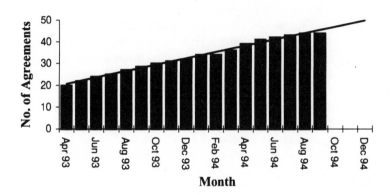

The choice of suppliers is critical. The whole EDI system works on the premise that there is guaranteed supply. In effect the supplier takes on the long-term, material planning to ensure that the supply pipeline is always full. In general terms the supplier guarantees 60 days worth of 'Kanbans' to always be available, and manages the horizon beyond based on forecast demand from the buyer.

For EDI replenishment to be successful a strong, open relationship is required. Buying on a 'spot' price cannot succeed in this type of replenishment environment. The level of detailed planning in implementing such a system cannot be under estimated.

Material Control Strategy - Simplified Logistics

The key elements of the above strategy were clearly derived from the problems previously explained and are:

- Cycle Time Reduction
- Reduce 'non-value' Adding Activities
- Reduce Inventory Levels

Traditional methods of component supply to the electronic assembly areas use a great deal of time and effort to schedule parts and require commitments from Avery Berkel to their suppliers to buy parts months in advance of their delivery and requirement. Keeping large stocks of parts is no guarantee of having the right parts, the obsolescence risk is high as are the costs associated with holding inventory. If we are able to communicate our requirements to suppliers effectively, then they can respond faster and we do not need to keep such large stocks of parts. A Kanban system (or two-bin system) of ordering can help in controlling the supply of parts by ensuring that only those parts used are re-ordered. If the quantities in the bins are kept to a practical, fixed minimum then storage problems (costs and physical area) can be reduced as well.

Both Kanban and two-bin require the supplier to receive a material notification to replenish the stock of the bin, either in the form of a label or an empty bin. This, obviously, requires transportation by post, carrier or other means, and can work out to be expensive and still take several days just to place the order.

Using EDI, the Kanban label can be 'delivered' instantly by telephone and fed directly into the supplier's order system. With the correct procedures set up at the supplier's dispatch department, parts used today can be replaced tomorrow. This means that stocks of components can be reduced whilst the flexibility of a process is retained. Smaller stocks mean that a greater variety of parts can be stocked in a convenient place.

This is the way the Avery Berkel EDI-Kanban system operates. Components are stocked where they will be needed, in manageable quantities, mostly around a week's usage in each bin. Each bin location has a bar coded Kanban label. This is the key to the part details and it eliminates mistakes in entering the order. All the information that the supplier requires is held on the computer which constructs the 'label' message that is telephoned to the supplier. The way in which this is done makes communication quick, effective and guaranteed. We can be sure that the supplier has received our order in the same way as using registered post.

SMT Cell Set-up

Speed and flexibility in production are the essence of the project, and the whole SMT department was set up to be able to produce small numbers of boards at short notice to support Kanban supply to the main product assembly department.

The placement machines were set up so that every surface mount component used in all Avery Berkel products is permanently mounted on the machine. The only requirement, when changing production from one board to another, is to load the correct unpopulated board and change the programme in the machine. Because the machine uses standard reels and 'sticks' of components, and since demand for any particular product can fluctuate, it was decided to supply the components to the machine from bins beside the machine, where any component could be found. The EDI Kanban system was adopted to supply the bins and prevent stock-outs, whilst keeping a modest number of parts.

People

The implementation of EDI came after large scale redundancies at Avery Berkel and there was great concern within the material control teams that this method would result in redundancies. However, this was not the intention. What was intended was the release of the team from performing mundane, high intensity low value tasks, to tasks that added greater value to the business. The choice of system and how it has been set up has been very much determined by the user community. There has been tremendous acceptance of the use of the system within the production cell.

Choice of EDI System

System Appraisal

A number of fact finding visits were made by representatives of Avery Berkel to assess the success of other companies with inventory and production control methods, in particular their use of EDI and Kanban.

System Trials

Two systems which ran in parallel, were selected for trial. Both systems were equal in technical capability so the choice was left with the end user. The decision on which system to implement was made before the full commissioning of the SMT department, in order to give sufficient time to install the hardware and accompanying bins of components. The decision was based on the following criteria:

- ease of use
- support and documentation
- integration with other existing company systems and software
- cost to implement, support and expand
- use and acceptance by trading partners

After a period of 2 months the POURS system supplied by Avnet EMG Value Added Service Group was chosen as the preferred platform.[*]

Hardware Costs

The equipment used in the POURS EDI Kanban system is shown in Table 11.1 and Table 11.2 below, with the purchase price. We shall not cover the detailed use or the functions of each piece.

Table 11.1 Equipment

Item	Specification	Cost
Personal Computer	Minimum 386/20, Hard drive, 3.5" floppy, monitor, two serial ports, one parallel, mouse and AT keyboard.	£500.00
Psion HC100	including mains adapter, rechargeable battery, serial interface and cable.	£407.50
Psion Cradle	suitable for HC100	£170.00
Laser Gun	with interface to Psion HC100	£595.00
Modem	Minimum 2400 baud, supplied by Avnet	£250.00
Printer	Laserjet compatible	£600.00

The only hardware not purchased for the project was the PC, as we had a number of under-utilised machines available.

Table 11.2 Software

Application	Specification	Cost
POURS Softa ordering	EDI enabling software/Psion HC100 software for barcode reading	£2000
Novell Netware	Connectivity to Local Area Network	Available Co. wide
GEIS	Connection Value Added Network	£600
GEIS	Transmission cost	£0.01/1000 characters

Total hardware and software costs, as capital expenditure, amounted to £4622.50

Training

A training document has been written to support the POURS EDI system and to provide the surface mount team with a reference manual on how to operate the DOS version of POURS. A good overview of the system is provided to demonstrate how all the elements fit together but, by providing on-the-job training and constant support and assistance in initial stages, the team soon adopted POURS and expansion of the system through EA&T has been rapid and user driven.

The EDI-Kanban setup at Avery Berkel

The EDI-Kanban system is based around a Personal Computer running Avnet VAS (Value Added Services) POURS software (POURS is DOS based menu driven EDI enabling software). Part and order details are kept in Dbase 3.0 files and can be interrogated by any software capable of handling such files. Barcodes are used via Psion HC100's and cradles with the supplied software. Barcode labels and documents can be printed on any 'Laserjet' compatible printer. The software has six levels of security and is capable of sending EDIFACT purchase orders (version 91.2) and receiving an acknowledgement based on the same message.

The messages sent constitute a call-off from an established blanket order. This represents the Kanban ticket and as such is placed directly on the suppliers 'Kanban board', their sales order system. The message itself contains all the data drawn from the POURS EDI database, wrapped in an envelope of additional characters that assist in interpretation by the recipient.

The PC contains its own independent database of part details: part number, description, bin location, supplier, etc.; the primary key to which is the unique bin-location code. Linked to this, also, are the Kanban quantity, order number, vendor code and other details as required.

Each bin of components has a label giving the part number description and its unique location number which is also barcoded. Using a barcode reader on bins that are empty or below their minimum stock quantity, the POURS system can construct a purchase order from the details in the database for use as an electronic Kanban ticket. This is then sent to the supplier of the part by means of a Value Added Network service (VAN) which acts as an electronic 'post office'.

Using the VAN means that all messages for all suppliers can be sent in one process, and will be redirected by the VAN service in a similar way to using a post box (each subscriber to the VAN service has his/her own mailbox: the routing between mailboxes is performed automatically by the VAN computer). Where a supplier cannot receive EDI messages, POURS will send a fax instead, maintaining many of the advantages of the system and allowing the two companies to progress at slightly differing speeds.

The relationship between the customer and the supplier has to be carefully planned and arranged to ensure that the supplier can provide the level of service that the low stock holding requires. The supplier puts sufficient stock in place in order to respond to any fluctuations in the call off from the Kanban pull system without delay and the customer needs to be able to give the supplier a prompt indication of expected changes in requirements for a part. The system is shown schematically in figure 11.4.

Figure 11.4: EDI Kanban at Avery Berkel

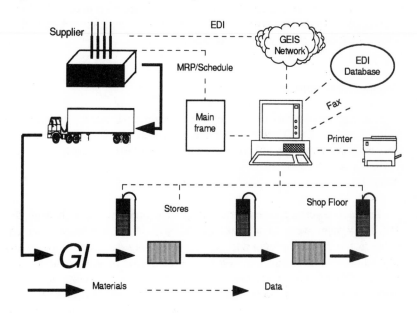

Preparation in Stores

Some of the parts used in the surface mount area are also used in other areas of the company's operations. Where this is the case and also when a supply of a component has changed to EDI but stocks are high, the vendor of the part will be indicated as Avery Berkel's own stores. An Ethernet point was installed in the stores and a printer and 'Pocket Print Server' connected to it, in order to print the POURS picking lists directly into the stores.

This enables the storeman to collect the picking list containing details of the Kanban requirements, including stores location, quantity, part number and a barcode for receiving the goods, and to make up the consignment for delivery into the surface mount area before the next morning. The same procedure is used for parts designated as supplier 'Preform' except that the storeman made up the consignment from the preform section and delivered it in the same way. Parts in the stores can be ordered by true EDI (when a part is in stores because it is shared) or by normal stock control procedures when a supplier is not an EDI or faxban supplier.

Another advantage of operating by this method is that for the operators in the surface mount area there is only one way of obtaining parts. They need not concern themselves with who is supplying the part and whether they should look for it in stores or goods inwards.

Problems Encountered

The largest problem to be overcome is the resource needed to interface POURS to the ICL OMAC mainframe environment. This represents the only major problem and affects both ordering and receiving parts.

Ordering

In practice most problems associated with ordering parts through the POURS system were as a result of the lack of an automatic interface between the POURS system and the manufacturing database. This means that all orders placed and sent to suppliers using EDI have to be updated on the ICL OMAC system manually. Whilst this does not create additional work, since orders would be placed under any system, it does mean that there is an additional time constraint on achieving this (next day for deliveries) and it leaves the system open to keying errors internally. The result of this is a failure to eliminate all goods receiving queries on parts, although the number has been reduced and the rate of clearing is much faster than previously.

Receiving

The POURS system incorporates an audit trail of all orders made from the time of initial entry in the system until receipt of the goods and closure of the loop. The problems seen in receiving goods are also mostly connected with the lack of an interface to the mainframe mentioned above. This is intended to allow the use of barcoded labels on the components when they arrive in goods inwards and will allow the automatic updating of goods received and stock transfer transactions. Parts ordered from stores will also benefit from this as the current manual stock transfer transaction can be performed as a result of the barcode printed on the picking list. It was expected that there might be a potential problem in receiving only partial shipments of goods, but this has not arisen in practice.

The interface required has been requested but is awaiting the availability of resource from the IT department responsible for maintenance of the mainframe computer. The link will be a simple file transfer and overnight batch update of purchase order call-off's and is expected to be in place within the next two to four months.

People

No job losses have occurred as a result of the introduction of the EDI system, in fact, the result has been an improvement in the standard of work and control achieved by the people who were concerned about their positions. As a result of the automation provided by POURS for ordering and the reduction in expediting tasks, time has been made available to schedulers and expediters to concentrate on the real problems and not the day to day running items which, previously, had to be continuously checked. Some items that were previously a problem to schedule have been moved to EDI Kanban and these have not caused any difficulties since. Staff affected find that they now have more time available for the jobs that others thought they were doing anyway!

Benefits

As mentioned in the introduction and throughout the article the benefits have been quite startling. Even though we have only focused on a small area of our manufacturing organisation, the potential for improvement is huge. As a result of the implementation of the development strategies and the introduction of POURS EDI Kanban we have achieved the following:

- Increasing stock turns nearly threefold (and still rising) (see figure 11.5).

Figure 11.5:

Surface Mount Production Cell - Stockturns

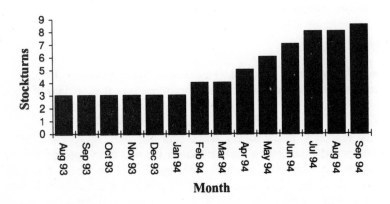

The initial static position was due to the consumption of in-house stocks.

- Inventory reduction of £220K (£440K to £220K) (see figure 11.6).
- Virtual elimination of production shortages. We have had one since implementation, when the line stopped!
- Improved communications
- Improved relationships with key suppliers
  - Payments are made more promptly
  - There are fewer administration problems
  - There are fewer quality problems
- Reducing non value activities such as scheduling, kitting and expediting
- Reduction in unit prices of components, savings in excess of £200K
- Return on investment of approx 90 times in the first year
- Greater job satisfaction for the staff involved
- Barcoding removing causes of error
- Demand driven replenishment at the point of consumption
- Replenishment to the Point of Use, cutting out internal stores

The effort taken to ensure that the whole system works should not be underestimated. To get this far it has been necessary to work extremely hard both internally and externally with our component suppliers. The results speak for themselves and are certainly worth the effort required.

Figure 11.6:

Surface Mount Production Cell Stock Value/£K

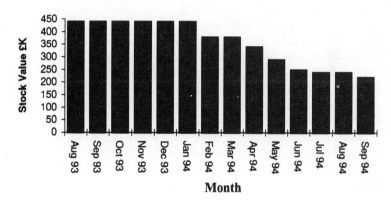

The future

Avery Berkel is just a very small step down the road in its use of EDI. There are many more ways in which EDI and its interface with our other business systems can be improved.

The main areas to look at are:

1. Other Production Areas

The POURS EDI Kanban system will be expanded to incorporate the whole of the Electronic Assembly and Test Department. This is planned to be completed by June 1995 and POURS has also been introduced into the Product Assembly department, but utilising the Faxban facility. The broadening of the use will be achieved using a network of Psion HC100's communicating with a networked copy of POURS. Software upgrades from Avnet are imminent and will result in POURS running under MS-Windows 3.1 so that pooling of Psions and EDI communications can be achieved simultaneously with other functions. Avery Berkel has around 8,000 live parts on its manufacturing database; only 1,000 are currently being ordered using EDI Kanban in the SMT cell and only 400 parts are ordered externally directly via EDI. There is still a long way to go.

2. Business Systems

One of the main remaining problems is that POURS is currently a stand-alone system. The plan is to integrate it into our ICL OMAC environment by the end of the current financial year. This will allow for the automatic generation and receiving of deliveries into POURS and OMAC with a simultaneous transaction. This will also allow the development of 'self invoicing' which is the next logical step. Problems currently experienced will be resolved by the introduction of a batch update link to the mainframe. This will eliminate all manual transactions related to parts ordering and stock transfer and will enable the implementation of automatic barcoded goods inwards receipts.

Another planned step is to generate the delivery forecasts, currently sent to suppliers monthly, and to format them in such a way that they too can be sent via EDI. This is planned for implementation within the next six months.

3. Other Business Areas

With the possibility of 'self invoicing' the opportunities for EDI within our Finance Department become apparent. This is probably the next major area of opportunity within our business. Although there are currently no timescales for the introduction of 'self invoicing', realistically it is 18-24 months away.

Conclusions

The benefits of implementing EDI Kanban have been widespread and are largely quantifiable. The whole approach has had a major impact on the production flexibility of the SMT cell and kept inventory in this area under control. Surface Mounted PCBs can be requested by Product Assembly in the morning and delivered by the afternoon, and batch sizes can be as low as one!

Avery Berkel consider this approach to integrating Purchasing and Material control strategies to be highly successful but it is not unique. Having identified the many problems in existence two years ago, our approach has enabled us to reduce non-value adding activities.

We have been cautious in the implementation process so that EDI Kanban has now become a normally accepted practice within our business and staff, at all levels, can clearly see the benefits. It is wise to be cautious in implementation because if the supply chain dries up production does stop very quickly.

In other companies, where the planning and procurement functions may be more advanced, there is still considerable scope for the use of EDI Kanban to reap similar benefits to those at Avery Berkel. If we had been more advanced we would probably have sent purchase orders/delivery schedules via EDI first and then moved to a replenishment system. For expediency we chose the route described above.

We would strongly recommend the practice of EDI Kanban because of its simplicity. It takes material demand at the point of use and converts it into a replenishment message. The supply chain is, as a result, shorter and staff are released to add value to material/purchasing processes as a whole.

---

* POURS is trade mark product of Avnet-EMG.